The Neue Pinakothek
Munich

The

Neue Pinakothek

Munich

Christian Lenz

C.H. BECK / SCALA PUBLISHERS

© Scala Publishers Ltd., London
in association with Verlag C.H. Beck oHG, Munich
© VG Bild-Kunst, Bonn 2003: Pierre Bonnard,
Maurice Denis, James Ensor, Max Liebermann,
Aristide Maillol, Edvard Munch, Pablo Picasso, Paul
Signac, Edouard Vuillard.

First published in 1989 by
Scala Publishers Limited
Gloucester Mansions
140a Shaftesbury Avenue
London WC2H 8HD

Revised and updated 2003

ISBN 3 406 51272 7 (C. H. Beck) / 1 85759 309 x (Scala)

Photography by the photographic department of the
Bayerische Staatsgemäldesammlungen, Munich and
Artothek, Weilheim
Translated from the German by Anthony Vivis, Tinch
Minter and Martin Chalmers
Designed by Andrew Shoolbred and Greg Taylor
Printed and bound by CS Graphics, Singapore

FRONT COVER ILLUSTRATION
Vincent van Gogh
Vase with sunflowers, 1888

BACK COVER ILLUSTRATION
Max Liebermann
Munich beer garden , 1883/84

FRONTISPIECE
Gustav Klimt
detail of *Music*, 1895

Contents

Introduction

The Neue Pinakothek is one of the several important museums which constitute the Bayerische Staatsgemäldesammlungen, or Bavarian State Collections. Its holdings amount to about 5,000 works of art, dating from the mid-eighteenth century to the early twentieth, with an emphasis on paintings and sculpture of the nineteenth century. About 550 works are on display.

Like the Alte Pinakothek (Old Master Gallery), the Neue Pinakothek (New Picture Gallery) was founded by King Ludwig I of Bavaria (born 1786, reigned 1825–48, died 1868). As Crown Prince (1799–1825), Ludwig took an active interest in contemporary art, especially German art, and before his accession he managed to influence its direction, pushing through the construction of the Glyptothek (Sculpture Gallery) from 1816 until its completion in 1830, and the appointments of Leo von Klenze as court architect in 1820 and of Peter Cornelius as director of the Munich Academy of Arts in 1824. As soon as he became King, Ludwig I enthusiastically initiated a wide range of projects, involving himself in architecture, town-planning and the purchase and commission of works of art. For Munich, the most important results of his activity were the creation of the Königsplatz (1816–48), the extension of the Residenz (1826–35) and the construction *ex novo* of the Alte Pinakothek (1826–36), the Allerheiligen-Hofkirche (Royal Church of All Saints, 1826–37), the Universitätskirche Sankt Ludwig (University Church of St Louis, 1829–43) and, rather later, the Neue Pinakothek (1846–53).

From his days as Crown Prince, Ludwig had frequent contact with artists, indeed he felt himself to be an artist. He acquired his first contemporary picture, a *Penitent Magdalen* by Heinrich Füger, in 1808. Among German artists, he especially favoured members of the German community in Rome. 'The Fine Art of painting, which lay extinguished, has been rekindled in the nineteenth century by Germans ...', declared Ludwig at the laying of the foundation stone of the Neue Pinakothek. His patronage was characterised by a passion for Italy and by strong patriotism, which the recent struggle against Napoleon may partly explain.

The Neue Pinakothek was not Munich's first institution for the promotion of contemporary art. The Kunstakademie (Academy of Arts) had been founded in

1

Aristide Maillol
Banyuls-sur-Mer 1861–1944 Banyuls-sur-Mer
Flora, 1910–12
Signed
Bronze, 163.5 cm high (including base)
Inv. no. B.154
Acquired in 1931 from the Wolff collection, Munich

This figure and three other statues constitute a cycle of the Four Seasons, which Maillol executed on commission from the Russian collector Morosoff.

2

Auguste Rodin
Paris 1840–1917 Meudon
Alexandre Falguière, 1899
Bronze, 44 cm high
Inv. no. B. 67
Acquired in 1913 at the international
art exhibition in the Glaspalast,
Munich

Alexandre Falguière (Toulouse
1831–1900 Paris) was a painter and
sculptor. He was a student of Albert-
Ernest Carrier-Belleuse, Jean-Louis
Chenillon and François Jouffroy. He
made his debut in the Salon of 1857
and was awarded the Prix de Rome
in 1859. On returning to Paris in 1867,
he had his greatest successes in the
Salon of that year, followed by
numerous commissions in the
following decades. Although both
Rodin and Falguière entered the
competition for the Balzac
Memorial, they were relatively close.
Rodin's bust of the older sculptor
has a counterpart in Falguière's
portrait of the younger man.

2

1808, not only to provide tuition and to exhibit its members' work but also more broadly 'as a centre of all artistic endeavour', which would have 'an artistically stimulating effect on the cultural life of the nation', according to Schelling's foundation charter. The Kunstverein (Art Union) was founded in 1823, with a membership primarily of landscape and genre painters who wished to challenge the authority of the Akademie. In 1838 Ludwig had promoted the construction of the Kunst- und Industrie-Ausstellungsgebäude (Halls for the Display of Arts, Crafts and Machines), intending to co-ordinate Akademie and Kunstverein exhibitions as international events which would rival those of Paris and Brussels. Ludwig began to plan for the construction of the Neue Pinakothek, and to collect art systematically to that end, in the 1830s.

When the Neue Pinakothek was opened in 1853, some 300 paintings could be exhibited, among which were important items from Leo von Klenze's collection, which Ludwig had acquired in 1841. The majority of works were genre or landscape, bought on the open market or at exhibitions of the Kunstverein. For the most part the history painters of the Akademie received patronage in commissions for public buildings: Peter von Cornelius and his team in the Glyptothek, the Alte Pinakothek and the Ludwigskirche, Schnorr von Carolsfeld in the Residenz, Heinrich Hess and the Schraudolph brothers in the Allerheiligen-Hofkirche; Ludwig also

3

3
Carl Rottmann
Handschuhsheim/Heidelberg
1797–1850 Munich
Marathon, 1848
Encaustic on stonecast,
157 × 200 cm
Inv. no. WAF 860
Acquired in 1845

This picture is one of a cycle of landscapes of Greece, produced between 1838 and 1850 for King Ludwig I. Encaustic, the medium in which Rottmann executed the pictures, had recently been developed in Munich. The cycle comprised 32 pictures and was originally intended for the arcades of the Hofgarten. Reduced to 23 landscapes, it finally found a home in a gallery of its own within the Neue Pinakothek.

commissioned Wilhelm von Kaulbach to make designs for the decoration of the Neue Pinakothek building.

Designs for the Neue Pinakothek were initiated in 1842. Abandoning his original idea to erect a building on the Gasteig, the King acquired a plot north of the Alte Pinakothek in 1845, and he laid the foundation stone on 12th October 1846. Friedrich von Gärtner's plans were amended and the new building was carried out by August Volt, one of Gärtner's pupils. The Museum was opened on 25th October 1853. It was a square-cut, largely windowless edifice, 107 metres long and 29 metres wide, rising to 27 metres high. It was conceived as a basilica, with a 'nave' rising 5 metres above the 'aisles'. It was decorated on the outside with vast frescoes, running the whole perimeter of the upper storey and depicting, in accordance with Ludwig's commission, '... recent developments in the Arts, called into being by *His Majesty the King*, and emanating from Munich'. The frescoes were executed by Christoph Nilson from Wilhelm von Kaulbach's designs.

The Neue Pinakothek was the first public museum in Europe devoted exclusively to contemporary art. Following Ludwig's death in 1868, the authorities began making new purchases in the 1880s. In 1891 Conrad Fiedler donated a large and important group of works by Hans von Marées. Between 1911 and 1913, came the Tschudi Donation, which included works by Manet, Rodin, Cézanne, van Gogh and Gauguin, among others, given by several benefactors as a memorial to the late Hugo von Tschudi, former Director of the Galleries. In 1915 the Neue Pinakothek came

under State control. As a result, in 1919, the more recent pictures were transferred to the Neue Staatsgalerie (now the Staatsgalerie Moderner Kunst, the State Gallery of Modern Art), but in 1981 they were returned to the rebuilt Neue Pinakothek. Since 1945, acquisition by the State has continued to be augmented by the generosity of private donors, who sometimes also make works available to the Gallery on long-term loan.

So great was the damage to King Ludwig's building in 1945 that it was decided to demolish it and construct another on the site. The foundation stone of the second building, designed by Alexander von Branca, was laid on 16th July 1975, and the Museum was opened on 28th March 1981. Models of the original and present Neue Pinakothek are displayed on the first floor and give the visitor a good idea of both buildings. All in all, the Neue Pinakothek presents itself to the visitor as a well laid-out museum building that functions well. In a deeper sense, by linking the principles of structure and hierarchy to tradition, the building establishes a clear analogy in the mind of the visitor, which can in turn guide him or her through the collection.

Anyone walking through the Museum will obtain a clear impression of developments in art from the middle of the eighteenth century to the beginning of the twentieth. The visitor will notice not only the differences between 'schools' and individual artists but also a divide between works, sometimes of great historical interest or importance, that were typical of their period or highly successful in their own day and other works that conform better to our own understanding of what makes great art. The visitor may choose to reflect on the fact that artists such as Cézanne, van Gogh, Marées and Leibl achieved little or no recognition in their own lifetime.

The range of the collection is apparent in the entrance hall. Sculptures by Aristide Maillol and Auguste Rodin and four paintings from Carl Rottmann's *Greece* series are examples, on the one hand, of a national and, in particular, Munich art that was current in the reign of Ludwig I. On the other hand, there are also examples of an international art, which is represented further by numerous important paintings and sculptures on display in the Gallery.

Théodore Géricault, detail of *Heroic landscape with fishermen* (plate 46)

International Art Around 1800

Art produced around 1800 documents the great disruption that occurred at the time of the French Revolution and affected all spheres of culture, including the arts. The French Revolution was not, of course, the cause of these far-reaching changes, but rather their expression. Before 1789 there had already been a reaction against the artificialities of Rococo, and 'nature' had emerged as the new artistic ideal. In their pursuit of this ideal, artists had begun to seek an immediate response to the landscape, and in the human sphere they upheld honesty, charity and other such 'natural' virtues, both of the individual and of society, in pictures that were often explicitly moralistic.

In this section there is a large number of English paintings, although English paintings have been acquired systematically by the Museum only during the last few decades. There has been a growing awareness that this 'school' was not simply under-represented (in this Gallery and on the Continent in general), but also had vital relevance to the development of European painting. These works are in many ways traditional – portraits reflecting the heritage of van Dyck, landscapes in the mode of Claude, or even paintings responding to the more recent French trends set by Watteau, Mercier and Gravelot. In other ways they reveal a new relationship to nature, above all in the new immediacy with which landscapes are painted and subjects are set within landscapes. A significant factor in this development was the English landscape garden as it evolved from about 1730, which certainly influenced landscape painting.

Almost all the important English painters of the eighteenth and nineteenth centuries are represented: there is a portrait by William Hogarth, otherwise known as a painter and engraver of moral tales, and pictures by George Stubbs, master painter of horses, by Sir Joshua Reynolds, first President of the Royal Academy and the author of an important *Discourses* on art, and by his rival Thomas Gainsborough, who besides his numerous portraits also painted many landscapes, in which he combined the influence of Claude with that of seventeenth-century Dutch art. There are also important examples of portraiture, so dominant in British art of the period, by George Romney, Henry Raeburn and Thomas Lawrence, who

Francisco José Goya y Lucientes, detail of *A party in the countryside* (plate 14)

4

4
Antonio Canova
Possagno 1757–1822 Venice
Paris, 1807–16
Marble, 205 cm high
Inv. no. WAF B.4
Acquired from the artist by Crown
Prince Ludwig in 1816

Paris, a son of Priam, King of Troy,
was called upon to decide which of
three goddesses, Hera, Athena and
Aphrodite, was the most beautiful.
He chose Aphrodite, and in return
received Helen as his wife, which
triggered the Trojan War.

were active primarily in the second half of the eighteenth century but lived on into the nineteenth. The landscapists John Constable and Joseph Mallord William Turner were also born in the eighteenth century, but their careers belong mostly to the nineteenth. Constable has exceptional importance in the history of landscape painting, since his influence was not only native but European; his plain straightforward vision of nature and use of unmixed colours made a great impression on Delacroix and the Barbizon School, and thus on many others influenced by their ideas. Constable and Turner had an important precursor in Richard Wilson, whose *View over the Thames* (plate 7), full of feeling though it is simply a 'view', is one of the most impressive landscapes in the collection.

French art of the period is represented by an outstanding picture by Jacques-Louis David, his portrait of the Marquise de Sorcy de Thélusson (plate 11). The leading French painter of his day, David harnessed the new interpretations of the Antique, which had been suggested by the rise of archaeology and by the writer Winckelmann and the painter Mengs, to the ideal then current of individual self-determination that recognised moral and social obligations. David's bold and radically simple work, in all its immediacy, is a remarkable example of the modern trend in art. On view in the annex, Anton Raphael Mengs' self-portrait and Heinrich Füger's portrait of Joseph Karl Stieler share David's approach to an extent.

The most important and varied painter of the period was Francisco de Goya y Lucientes, court painter to the Spanish King Charles IV from 1789. His paintings include both religious and genre scenes (mostly cartoons for tapestries), though the majority are portraits, and he is equally famous for his moralizing graphic work (*Caprichos*, 1797–98, *Desastres de la Guerra* 1810–20), in which he excoriated human weakness and suffering. Despite the fact that Goya developed in the milieu of Italian and Spanish art between Baroque and Neoclassicism, he was a realist painter who drew inspiration from Velázquez and Rembrandt. His pictures, whether profound characterisations, sarcastic journalism or possessed visions, have an intensity no contemporary matched. The Neue Pinakothek owns ten of his paintings, including a rare still life.

Besides the many paintings in this section Antonio Canova's statue of *Paris* should be mentioned, as it captures the Italian Neoclassicist's sensitivity.

5

Sir Joshua Reynolds
Plympton Earl's 1723–1792 London
Captain Philemon Pownall, 1769
Canvas, 233 × 148 cm
Inv. no. 14932
Acquired in 1985 from L. Herner,
Zurich

Philemon Pownall was born and
grew up in Plymouth. He entered
the Royal Navy as a young man and
served as a lieutenant under
Admiral Boscawen. On 5th June
1780, as commander of the frigate
Apollo, he was killed in a naval
engagement with the Spanish
frigate *Stanislaus*.

6

Sir Thomas Lawrence
Bristol 1769–1830 London
The sons of the first Lord Talbot, c. 1792
Canvas, 228.7 × 212.8 cm
Inv. no. 14882
Acquired in 1984 with the aid of the
Ernst von Siemens art fund

The subjects are Charles Chetwynd-
Talbot, Viscount Ingestre, and his
younger brother, the Hon. John
Chetwynd-Talbot, in the grounds of
the family seat, Hensol Castle,
overlooking Cardiff Bay.

5

6

7

8

7
Richard Wilson
Penegoes 1714–1782 Colommendy
View over the Thames at Kew Gardens
towards Syon House, 1760–70
Signed
Canvas, 104 × 138.5 cm
Inv. no. 14559
Acquired in 1978

8
Henry Fuseli
Zurich 1741–1825 London
Satan and Death, divided by Sin,
1792–1802
Canvas, 91.3 × 711.1 cm
Inv. no. 9494
Acquired in 1928 on the Munich art
market

This is a scene from John Milton's
Paradise Lost (II, 702 ff), a work
which Fuseli illustrated in other
pictures and which also occupied
other artists, including William
Blake.

9

10

9
Thomas Gainsborough
Sudbury 1727–1788 London
Mrs Thomas Hibbert, 1786
Canvas, 127 × 101.5 cm
Inv. no. FV 4
Acquired in 1978 by the Verein zur
Förderung der Alten und Neuen
Pinakothek

In 1784, Sophia Boldero (1760–1829)
had married Thomas Hibbert, who
came from a long-established
mercantile family in Manchester.

10
George Romney
Dalton 1734–1802 Kendal
Catherine Clements, 1788,
Signed
Canvas, 127.4 × 102.3 cm
Inv. no. HUW 29
Acquired in 1974 for the collection
of the Bayerische Hypotheken- und
Wechselbank

Catherine, the daughter of the Irish
statesman John Beresford, was
born in 1760. In 1788 she married
the Right Honourable Henry
Theophilus Clements. She died
in 1836.

11
Jacques-Louis David
Paris 1748–1825 Brussels
Marquise de Sorcy de Thélusson, 1790
Signed and dated
Canvas, 129 × 97 cm
Inv. no. HUW 21
Acquired in 1971 for the collection
of the Bayerische Hypotheken- und
Wechselbank

Anne-Marie-Louise Rilliet
(1770–1845), the eldest daughter of
a Geneva banker, was painted by
David shortly after her marriage to
the Marquis de Sorcy de Thélusson.
The commission came from her
uncle, for whom David also painted
the portrait of Anne-Marie-Louise's
aunt, his sister, Jeanne-Robertine,
later Marquise d'Orvillier (now in
the Louvre).

11

12

13

12

Francisco José Goya y Lucientes
Fuendetodos 1746–1828 Bordeaux
Don José Queraltó in the uniform of
Spanish military doctor, 1802
Signed and dated
Canvas, 101.5 × 76.1 cm
Inv. no. 9334
Acquired in 1925 on the Berlin art
market

Don José Queraltó, who was born
in Tarragona and died in Madrid in
1805, was a surgeon and writer, a
professor at the Real Colegio de
Medicina y Cirugia de San Carlos,
Madrid, and from 1793 onwards
director of the hospitals in Navarra
and Guipúzcoa. He is shown
wearing the uniform of a military
doctor with the rank of general.
Goya is reputed to have given
him the portrait in gratitude for
medical help.

13

Francisco José Goya y Lucientes
Fuendetodos 1746–1828 Bordeaux
Marquesa de Caballero, 1807
Signed and dated
Canvas, 104.7 × 83.7 cm.
Inv. no. HUW 13
Acquired in 1968 for the collection
of the Bayerische Hypotheken- und
Wechselbank

The sitter's full title was Doña Maria
Soledad de la Rocha Fernández de la
Peña, Marquesa de Caballero
(1774–1809). In 1795 she became lady-
in-waiting to Queen Maria Luisa of
Spain, and in 1800 she married the
Marqués de Caballero (1770–1821),
who was Spanish Minister of Justice
from 1798 to 1808. Goya painted a
portrait of her husband as a
pendant.

14
Francisco José Goya y Lucientes
Fuendetodos 1746–1828 Bordeaux
A party in the countryside, 1776
Canvas, 40.2 × 54.6 cm
Inv. no. HUW 23
Acquired in 1973 for the collection
of the Bayerische Hypotheken- und
Wechselbank

This picture was painted on
commission from the Marqués de
Montvirgen y San Carlo as a
memento of an excursion. It
possibly also served as a study for
a large cartoon, now lost, for a
tapestry. In 1776, Goya is known to
have supplied the royal tapestry
factory with a cartoon of the same
title, 'La Merienda Campestre'.

14

15
Francisco José Goya y Lucientes
Fuendetodos 1746–1828 Bordeaux
Doña Maria Teresa da Vallabriga,
c. 1783
Canvas, 151.2 × 97.8 cm
Inv. no. HUW 2
Acquired in 1966 for the collection
of the Bayerische Hypotheken- und
Wechselbank

In 1776, Maria Teresa (1758–1828)
married the Infante, Don Luis de
Borbón, sixth son of Philip V and
younger brother of Charles III.
Archbishop of Seville and Toledo,
and finally a Cardinal, he
relinquished orders so as to be able
to marry Doña María Teresa.

15

16

16
Sir David Wilkie
Cults 1785–1841 at sea
The Reading of the Will, 1820
Signed and dated
Panel, 76 × 115 cm
Inv. no. WAF 1194
Acquired by King Maximilian I of
Bavaria, for whom it was painted

The scene is taken from Walter
Scott's novel *Guy Mannering* and
follows the funeral of Lady
Singleside. Bannister had already
put it on the stage before Wilkie
took it as his subject, and when he
exhibited his painting at the Royal
Academy it was an immediate and
extraordinary success. Wilkie soon
became the most celebrated painter
of genre in England.

17
John Constable
East Bergholt 1776–1837 London
Dedham Vale seen from East Bergholt,
c. 1825
Canvas, 45.6 × 55.1 cm
Inv. no. FV 5
Acquired in 1982 by the Verein zur
Förderung der Alten und Neuen
Pinakothek

Constable had a studio built in the
grounds of the mill his parents
owned in East Bergholt. To paint
this view, the artist evidently took
up a standpoint some 300 metres
south-west of the studio.

18
Joseph Mallord William Turner
London 1175–1851 London
Ostend, 1844
Canvas, 91.8 × 122.3 cm
Inv. no. 14435
Acquired in 1976 on the London art
market

17

18

German Classicism and Romanticism

EARLY ROMANTICISM

This section features mainly German painting of the early nineteenth century, with important examples from the main centres of Dresden, Berlin and Munich. Strictly the term 'Romantic' applies only to some of the works, and even for these it is more a tag than a proper description.

Dresden had become one of the artistic capitals of Europe in the eighteenth century, and, though most famous for its Baroque achievements, it also contributed to the rise of Neoclassicism. The archaeological writer Johann Joachim Winckelmann and Anton Raphael Mengs (whose self-portrait is in Room 2a) spent formative years there, and Winckelmann published his *Reflections on the Imitation of the Greek Arts* in Dresden in 1755. Around 1800, there was an important circle of Dresden-based Romantic writers – Schelling, the Schlegel brothers, Novalis, Tieck and Wackenroder – whose work in general drew inspiration from the city's collection of paintings and its beautiful countryside, and some of whom participated in discussion about the visual arts (for instance, Wilhelm Wackenroder's *Heartfelt Effusions of an Art-loving Monk*, 1797, or August Wilhelm and Caroline von Schlegel's collection of essays entitled *Paintings*, 1799). Of the painters active in Dresden at this time, the most important was Caspar David Friedrich. Having completed his studies at the Copenhagen Academy, Friedrich settled in the city in 1798, and had as associates Carl Gustav Carus, Georg Friedrich Kersting and the Norwegian-born Johan Christian Clausen Dahl, among others of lesser rank. Friedrich's art is characterised by its religious feeling, which was widespread among the early Romantics, and its nationalism, which had been aroused by Germany's political and military conflict with France. His landscapes show a deep feeling for the richness of nature, and they often seem not merely observed but actually experienced. Friedrich's tendency towards symbolism, the belief conveyed by his landscapes that 'a man's reach should exceed his grasp', and his conception of the cyclical nature of life set him apart from the more factual, sometimes unimaginative outlook of Dahl or even of Karl Blechen, a leading Berlin painter

Caspar David Friedrich, detail of *Summer* (plate 23)

who was on close terms with Friedrich. Kersting, unlike these men, was not so much a landscapist as a painter of everyday bourgeois life, whose small-scale works of great sensibility heralded Biedermeier painting of the middle decades of the nineteenth century.

The Munich 'school' is represented above all by Dillis, Kobell, Klenze and Rottmann, artists united by a common purpose to a much lesser extent than those in Dresden. Wilhelm von Kobell was a painter of serene landscapes, usually in a clear morning light, though he also specialised in battle-scenes and animal pictures. Carl Rottmann, born in Heidelberg, painted more dramatic landscape setpieces, which reached their fulfilment in his *Greece* cycle, inspired as much by Greece's history as by its terrain. The two works by Leo von Klenze (court architect from 1820) on view in the Gallery reveal his skills as an archaeologist and architect

19

19
Johan Christian Clausen Dahl
Bergen 1788–1857 Dresden
The day after a stormy night, 1819
Signed and dated
Canvas, 74.5 × 105.6 cm
Inv. no. 14631
Acquired in 1980 from a Norwegian
private collection

The artist considered this picture,
which he completed in eight days,
his best work. Contrary to the
opinion of Academic critics, he
believed that the viewer must have
experienced the hostile side of
nature in order to appreciate his
picture.

20
Georg Friedrich Kersting
Güstrow 1785–1847 Meissen
*Young woman sewing by the light of a
lamp*, 1828
Signed
Canvas, 40.3 × 34.2 cm
Inv. no. 14603
Acquired in 1979 from the Rudolf
Neumeister Gallery, Munich

20

21

22

21

Karl Blechen

Cottbus 1798–1840 Berlin

View of Assisi, c. 1830

Canvas, 97 × 146.3 cm

Inv. no. 10338

Acquired in 1937 from a private collection

Journeying from Rome in 1829, Blechen lingered in Assisi for several days, and he painted several versions of this view of the church of San Francesco. Back in Berlin, he worked up this large picture from sketches.

22

Karl Blechen

Cottbus 1798–1840 Berlin

The construction of the Devil's Bridge,
c. 1830

Canvas, 77.6 × 104.5 cm

Inv. no. L. 1039

On loan from the Federal Republic of Germany

On his way home, Blechen also made several sketches of the so-called Devil's Bridge at the St Gotthard Pass. He evidently painted this picture shortly afterwards.

23

24

23
Caspar David Friedrich
Greifswald 1774–1840 Dresden
Summer, 1807
Canvas, 71.4 × 103.6 cm
Inv. no. 9702
Acquired in 1931 on the Munich art
market

Friedrich painted a *Winter* as a
companion piece to this picture.
Seasonal landscapes of this kind
were favourite subjects of the artist.

24
Caspar David Friedrich
Greifswald 1774–1840 Dresden
Pine thicket in snow, c. 1828
Canvas, 30 × 24 cm
Inv. no. ESK 1
Acquired in 1983 for the collection
with the aid of the the Ernst von
Siemens art fund

Friedrich painted a companion
piece in this case also (*Trees and
bushes in snow*, Dresden).

25

26

26
Wilhelm von Kobell
Mannheim 1766–1835 Munich
View of the River Isar near Munich, 1819
Signed and dated
Panel, 40.5 × 53.5 cm
Inv. no. 9213
Acquired in 1924 from a private
collection

25
Wilhelm von Kobell
Mannheim 1766–1853 Munich
The Seige of Cosel, 1808
Signed and dated
Canvas, 202 × 305 cm
Inv. no. 3822
Passed from the private collection
of King Ludwig I to the State in 1832

This oil painting is one of a twelve-
part cycle which the Crown Prince
Ludwig had commissioned from
the painter. The cycle depicted
Bavaria's victories for the Rhenish
League against Prussia and Russia.
According to an inscription on the
reverse of the picture, this
represents the third breakout made
by the Prussian garrison from the
fortress of Cosel in Silesia. It was
repulsed on 15 March 1806 by the
Bavarians under Major General von
Raglovich.

27

Leo von Klenze

Schleden 1784–1864 Munich

The Acropolis of Athens, 1846

Signed and dated

Canvas, 102.8 × 147.7 cm

Inv. no. 9463

Acquired by King Ludwig I, and State property since 1927

In 1820, the architect Leo von Klenze was appointed Superintendent of Buildings in Bavaria. In 1834, he was sent on a diplomatic mission to Athens, where Ludwig's son, Otto, was King. While in Greece, he took an active interest in antiquities, taking detailed measurements of them and making provision for their special protection. He created this reconstruction of the Acropolis out of his detailed knowledge. This is one of a considerable number of impressive paintings by the architect.

27

28

Johann Georg von Dillis

Grüngiebing 1759–1841 Munich

The von Triva Palace, 1797

Signed and dated

Panel, 19 × 26.3 cm

Inv. no. 9392

Acquired in 1927 from a private collection in Starnberg

The small palace, which Privy Councillor von Ostwaldt had built in 1705 at one end of what is now Briennerstrasse (to the north of what was the Kapuzinergraben), was later owned by Privy Councillor von Triva. From 1785 onwards, it belonged to Karl Albert von Aretin, whose son Adam was taught to draw by Dillis. Dillis already had a close relationship with Ludwig when he was Crown Prince. In 1822, he became Director of the Central Art Gallery.

28

THE COURT ART OF LUDWIG I

Munich owes the position it attained in the nineteenth century as a leading centre of the arts in Europe largely to the energy of Ludwig I. This section (and also the neighbouring rooms) contain works by the artists most favoured by the King, portraits of the most important figures in his circle and works that depict the events in which he was involved, directly or indirectly. It includes, for example, Franz Catel's group portrait of Ludwig with German artists in Rome, as well as works by Peter von Hess that show scenes from the career of Ludwig's son, Otto, in Bavaria and as King of Greece. The portraits include that of Wilhelm von Schelling and Joseph Karl Stieler's of Goethe, one of the most penetrating likenesses of the poet ever made. Ludwig himself commissioned Stieler's portrait and many other pictures shown here, while he bought other works directly from artists or at exhibitions.

It is obvious from the works here and in adjoining sections, as from the King's activity as a collector and promoter, that his taste was accommodating and catholic, even to the point of contradiction. Ludwig could appreciate both the Antique and the Medieval, both Klenze's and Thorwaldsen's classicism and the Nazarenes' sentimentalism, and even the realist-genre work of a painter like Dillis, dedicated more to nature. He was nevertheless dogmatically committed to art, declaring at the laying of the foundation stone of the Neue Pinakothek, 'Art should not be regarded as a luxury. It has a part in every aspect of existence, it crosses over into life, and where there is no art there is no proper life. My great artists are my pride and my joy. The statesman's work will have long since passed away, while the creations of great artists continue to delight and to inspire.'

29

Franz Ludwig Catel

Berlin 1778–1856 Rome

Crown Prince Ludwig in the Spanish inn at Rome, 1824

Dated on the back on a slip of paper that identifies the men in the foreground of the composition

Canvas, 63 × 73 cm

Inv. no. WAF 142

From the private collection of Ludwig I

This shows the Crown Prince surrounded by German artists living in Rome. In a letter of 20 March 1824 to the art critic Gottlieb von Quandt, Catel wrote:

... I have just finished a small bambocciata for the Crown Prince of Bavaria. His Royal Highness had graciously arranged an intimate déjeuner at Don Raffaele's on the Ripa Grande, to mark Herr von Klenze's departure. He commanded me to immortalize the scene in paint... From left to right the subjects are: mine host, Crown Prince Ludwig, Thorvaldsen, Leo von Klenze, Count Seinsheim, Johann Martin Wagner (standing), Phillip Veit, Dr Ringseis (standing), Julius Schnorr von Carolsfeld, Catel, and Baron Gumppenburg. Through the open door the Aventine Hill on the far side of the Tiber can be seen...

29

30
Joseph Karl Stieler
Mainz 1781–1858 Munich
Johann Wolfgang von Goethe, 1828
Canvas, 78.2 × 63.8 cm
Inv. no. WAF 1048
Acquired in 1828 by King Ludwig I

This painting was commissioned by Ludwig I and painted in Weimar. The piece of paper in the poet's hand shows the first lines of a poem Ludwig had written in 1818:

Yes! Just as the flower Flora herself renews
Through the seed which she widely strews,
So one work of art succeeds another,
For life is mother to a new life;
Once feelings have become a work of art
Another splendid work through the strife
Of millennia will appeal to the heart.
Autumn, 1818. Ludwig.

31
Bertel Thorvaldsen
Copenhagen 1770–1844 Copenhagen
Adonis, 1808–32
Signed
Marble, 182 cm high
Inv. no. WAF-B.29
Acquired by King Ludwig I

Adonis the hunter was famous in Greek mythology for his beauty. Aphrodite, goddess of Love, and Persephone, goddess of the Dead, fought over him fiercely. It was settled that he should spend two thirds of the year on earth with Aphrodite, and the other third with Persephone in the Underworld. This symbolised the annual death and rebirth of nature.

Crown Prince Ludwig commissioned the statue from Thorvaldsen in 1808, but the sculptor did not complete it until 1832. This is one of the few works, if not indeed the only one, that he completed entirely by his own hand.

30

31

GERMAN CLASSICISTS IN ROME

Chronologically the first of the artists represented in this section is Jakob Philipp Hackert, who from 1768 lived in Rome, then in Naples and Florence. He knew Winckelmann and Mengs, and made the acquaintance of Goethe during the poet's travels in Italy. Goethe thought highly of him and arranged for his autobiography to be published in 1811. Hackert painted exact and detailed landscape views; for Goethe, his 'portraits of landscapes were perfect likenesses', and he praised his 'views', 'prospects' and 'illustrations', but distinguished them from landscapes proper, which for him were the ideal visions of Claude and Poussin.

Poussin and similar artists were again the point of reference for Joseph Anton Koch, who belonged to the generation that followed Hackert. Koch reached Rome in 1795, and while there he knew Johann Christian Reinhardt, Asmus Jacob Carstens and the Danish sculptor Thorwaldsen. Following the example of his teacher Adam Friedrich Oeser, Reinhardt painted heroic classical landscapes in the mode of Poussin and Claude, and in turn he influenced his slightly younger contemporary Koch, who set out to represent his experiences of the Swiss Alps in the style of Poussin and Gaspard Dughet. Koch combined numerous studies to create ambitious compositions such as *Schmadribachfall* (The Schmadribach waterfall) or *Heroic landscape with rainbow* (plate 34). Although he tackled Nature on a grand scale, individual details are closely observed and placed in relationship with the whole.

Koch is a significant figure in German art not only because of his classicizing tendencies but also his connections with the Nazarenes, whose interest in Early Renaissance Italian painting and religious subjects Koch shared. Between 1825 to 1829 he finished the cycle of paintings that the Nazarene Peter von Cornelius had begun, and Philipp Veit had continued, in the Sala Dante of the Casino Massimo in Rome. Koch was able to make his work available and impart his ideas to a number of students in Rome, among them the Dresden painter Ludwig Richter. After his *Heroic landscape* was bought in 1815 by the Munich Academy of Arts as an exemplary exercise in the genre, Koch influenced German artists in Germany, as well as Italy.

Richter completed the mountain landscape shown in the Gallery, *The Watzmann*, in 1894, a year after meeting Koch, and the influence of Koch's recently completed *Schmadribachfall* is clearly visible. In contrast to Koch's mature handling, which conveys the grandeur and gravity of the Alpine landscape, Richter's work has a prettier, altogether more bland and tranquil aspect. During the three years in which he remained in Italy, Richter was also drawn to Ernst Fries, a close contemporary who, after studying in Heidelberg and Munich, came to Rome in the same year, 1893. Fries was influenced not only by the circle of German artists in Rome but also by an Englishman, George Wallis, who had lived in Heidelberg from 1812 to 1816 and taught landscape-painting there both to Fries and to Carl Rottmann.

32
Ludwig Richter
Dresden 1803–1884 Dresden
The Watzmann, 1824,
Signed and dated
Canvas, 120.2 × 93 cm
Inv. no. 8983.
Acquired in 1918 from a private collection in Dresden.

The Watzmann is a range in the western-Salzburg or Upper-Austrian Alps in Bavaria, south-west of Berchtesgaden. Its highest peak attains 2713 metres.

This was the first major picture Richter painted after his arrival in Rome, in the autumn of 1823. He worked it up from travel sketches in the studio of Joseph Anton Koch. Koch's recently completed landscape *Schmadribachfall* may well have inspired him.

32

33

33
Jakob Philipp Hackert
Prenzlau 1737–1807 San Pietro di
Careggi
Lake Averno, 1794
Signed and dated
Paper mounted on card, 57.6 × 83.6 cm
Inv no. 10162
Acquired in 1936 from a private
collection

According to a description in an
exhibition catalogue of 1798, this
depicts 'an accurate view of Lake
Averno and the Gulf of Baia, from
the road which leads from Pozzuoli
to the Arco Felice and ancient
Cumae. . . in the foreground a
flowering aloe. . . The lake itself is
formed by the collapsed crater of a
volcano. On its left bank we see the
ruins of the Temple of Apollo, and
in the distance the castle of Baia and
the beautiful mountain of Miseno.
The scene is represented in the
radiance of a clear morning.'

34
Joseph Anton Koch
Obergibeln 1768–1839 Rome
Heroic landscape with rainbow, 1815
Signed and dated
Canvas, 188 × 171.2 cm
Inv. no. WAF 447
Acquired in 1850 by Ludwig I

This oil painting, which Koch
began as early as 1804, is the most
ambitious of a group of very
similar pictures. Shortly after its
completion, the Munich Academy
acquired it as a model of landscape
painting for the instruction of
student artists.

35

Rudolf (Ridolfo) Schadow
Rome 1786–1822 Rome
Woman tying her sandal, 1813 (1817)
Signed and dated
Marble, 118 cm high
Inv. no. WAF-B.24
Acquired by Crown Prince Ludwig

In this figure, Schadow combined
naturalism with the evocation of
famous antique sculptures such
as the *spinario* or the *fanciulla* (a
seated nymph) in the Uffizi,
Florence. It so impressed Schadow's
contemporaries that he had to make
seven replicas, of which this is one.

THE NAZARENES

'Nazarenes' was the Italians' derisive nickname for the young German artists who,
from 1810, lived as a quasi-monastic community in the former convent of
Sant'Isidoro in Rome, and grew their hair long in a manner reminiscent of Jesus of
Nazareth. A group of them – Friedrich Overbeck, Franz Pforr, Ludwig Vogel and
Konrad Hottinger – had been students at the Academy of Arts in Vienna, where in
1809 they had formed a 'Lukasbund', or Brotherhood of St Luke, deliberately
recalling medieval tradition. In opposition to the abstract and mechanical rules of
the Academy's classicistic teaching, the Brotherhood sought a renewal of artistic
tradition that was specifically Christian and specifically German. Those who moved
to Rome in the following year remained true to this endeavour.

Despite their rejection of academic classicism, the Nazarenes' ideals, style and
subject matter did not depart very far from it, even in their characteristic recourse
to Raphael and their efforts to synthesize German and Italian art. They had
absorbed much, including their nostalgia for the middle ages, their emphasis on
Germanness in art and their admiration for Raphael and Dürer, from writers of the
previous generation, such as Bodmer, Breitinger, Herder and Goethe, and artists
such as J. H. W. Tischbein. A step further was taken when several of the Nazarenes
converted to Catholicism, but even this had a parallel in the conversion of writers
such as Wackenroder and Tieck.

The essence of the Nazarene movement was its innocence, and its 'suffer the
little children' ideal of purity and tenderness. The Nazarenes sought to unmake the
history of art, and to escape its taint and corruption by return to first principles, as
represented by their 'divine' Raphael and their 'beloved' Dürer. Their paintings
reflected their hearts and minds, and their subjects were chosen or framed in such
a way as to avoid reference to the particular and the present, or indeed the real. It
was not long before the eye-catching simplicity of their work and its religious,
moral and nationalist appeal had brought the Nazarenes fame and success, and the
recognition they received continued to increase.

36

37

38

36
Friedrich Overbeck
Lübeck 1789–1869 Rome
Italia and Germania, 1828
Canvas, 94.4 × 104.7 cm
Inv. no. WAF 755
Acquired in 1832 by Ludwig I at its
exhibition in the Munich Academy

Overbeck designed this painting,
one of the Nazarenes' key works, as
an expression of his friendship for
Franz Pforr, who completed its
pendant, *Sulamith and Maria,*
shortly before his early death. At
that time, Overbeck had only
finished the cartoon, and he
produced the final version in 1828
for Wenner, a dealer in books and
art. The picture is an allegory of the
union between Germany and Italy,
and its subject matter is typical of
Nazarene art. The imitation of
Raphael's style and the painting's
delicacy are also characteristic of
the Nazarenes.

37
Friedrich Overbeck
Lübeck 1789–1869 Rome
Vittoria Caldoni da Albano, 1821
Canvas, 89 × 65.5 cm
Inv. no. WAF 757
Acquired in 1823 by Crown Prince
Ludwig

The sitter was the daughter of a
wine grower from Albano. She had
her portrait painted by numerous
artists, especially the Nazarenes, for
her face embodied their ideal of
beauty.

38
Wilhelm von Schadow
Berlin 1788–1862 Düsseldorf
A young Roman woman, 1818
Canvas, 94.3 × 73.1 cm
Inv. no. L267
Commissioned by Crown Prince
Ludwig. On loan from the
Verwaltung der staatlichen
Schlösser, Gärten und Seen, Munich
(Residenzmuseum Munich).

39

39
Heinrich Maria Hess
Düsseldorf 1798–1863 Munich
Marchesa Florenzi, 1824
Canvas, 192 × 139 cm
Inv. no. WAF 345
Commissioned by Crown Prince
Ludwig and acquired in 1824

The future King Ludwig I made the
acquaintance of the Marchesa
Marianna Florenzi in Rome in 1821.
From that time a very close
relationship developed between
them, accompanied by a
voluminous correspondence.
Ludwig also commissioned other
artists, including Joseph Karl Stieler
and Bertel Thorvaldsen, to make
portraits of the woman he so much
admired.

Biedermeier Art

The character Gottfried Biedermeier was invented by the writer Adolf Kussmaul in 1853. From 1855 to 1857 'Gedichte Biedermeiers' (Biedermeier Poems), written jointly by Kussmaul and Ludwig Eichenrodt, appeared regularly in the Munich satirical magazine *Münchner Fliegende Blätter* (Loose Munich Pages). Biedermeier was modelled on a real individual, Samuel Friedrich Sauter (1766–1846), a 'childlike, docile and simple-minded' teacher and poet, but Biedermeier stood for the typical German bourgeois of the period between the Congress of Vienna in 1815 and the March Revolution of 1848. In fact, the name Biedermeier has become synonymous with the period, with its arts and furniture and the lifestyle that prevailed in German-speaking countries and Denmark at that time. In literature, its leading representatives are Grillparzer, Stifter, Uhland and Mörike, and in art Ferdinand George Waldmüller, Moritz von Schwind and Carl Spitzweg, works by all of whom are shown in the Neue Pinakothek.

Biedermeier art is quintessentially bourgeois. It depicts ordinary middle-class life, with a greater or lesser degree of sentimentality, but always unheroically and without political comment. It eschews the high ideals of Neoclassical and Romantic academic history painting, and it is instead self-consciously unpretentious. Like the burghers' art of seventeenth-century Holland or art in the same vein produced more widely in Europe from the middle of the eighteenth century, Biedermeier art reflected the world with which its patrons felt at home as naturalistically as possible. It is most successful in and generally restricted to portraits (for example *Waldmüller's son Ferdinand with a dog*), landscapes (Waldmüller's *Zell-am-See in the Pinzgau*) and domestic scenes (Schwind's *The visit*). Given the propensity of most Biedermeier artists to sentimental moralising, anecdotal detail and sly touches of humour, domestic scenes were naturally their most popular subjects. Biedermeier art did not evolve in a vacuum, however, and it cannot be divorced from art as a whole, as Schwind's work alone demonstrates with its strong Romantic traits. The approach to nature of Spitzweg, and Waldmüller in his later landscapes, echoes the committed objectivity and dedication to nature of the French Barbizon School and their German equivalents who were active from the 1830s.

Moritz von Schwind detail of *The Visit* (plate 42)

40

41

40
Friedrich von Amerling
Vienna 1803–1887 Vienna
Young girl in a straw hat, c. 1835
Canvas, 59 × 47 cm
Inv. no. 9999
Acquired in 1935 on the Munich art
market

This fine example of the Viennese
school of Biedermeier painting
exists in several autograph versions.

41
Ferdinand Georg Waldmüller
Vienna 1793–1865 Hinterbrühl
*Waldmüller's son Ferdinand with a
dog,* 1836
Signed and dated
Panel, 39.2 × 31.2 cm
Inv. no. 9274
Acquired in 1925 on the Vienna art
market

The artist's son Ferdinand was born
in Brünn in 1816 and died in Vienna
in 1885.

42

42
Moritz von Schwind
Vienna 1804–1871 Niederpöcking
The visit, c. 1855
Canvas, 72 × 51 cm
Inv. no. 8120
Acquired in 1900 from the artist's estate

This painting is one of the artist's so-called 'travel pictures', small-scale works which Schwind produced in the 1850s and 1860s, when he had no purchasers for his large pictures.

43
Ferdinand Georg Waldmüller
Vienna 1793–1865 Hinterbrühl
Early spring in the Wienerwald, c. 1860
Signed and dated
Panel, 54.2 × 67.9 cm
Inv. no. 9324
Acquired in 1926 on the Munich art market

The picture belongs to a group of very similar subjects by Waldmüller.

44
Domenico Quaglio
Munich 1787–1837 Hohenschwangau
The Old Riding School with the Café Tambosi in 1822, 1822
Signed and dated
Canvas, 62 × 83 cm
Inv. no. WAF 786
Acquired by Ludwig I

This painting depicts the entrance into the Ludwigstrasse in Munich during its construction, looking north. In the left foreground, part of the façade of the Theatine church is visible with the so-called Lyre, or Lion Fountain, in front of it. In the right background, the Old Riding School, which was demolished in 1822, and the Baroque Café Tambosi at the Hofgarten can be seen.

43

44

Late Romanticism and Realism in France

The important works exhibited in this section are extremely varied, and comparatively few of them are embraced by the term 'Romantic'. All date from the early and middle nineteenth century, however, and in their own day most were progressive, that is they were not Academic or produced by Academicians, and in one way or another they anticipated elements of Impressionism.

Théodore Géricault and Eugène Delacroix were painters of complex, eventful, 'history' compositions of a kind that had no further development after Delacroix's death. The most important painter of the nineteenth century after Goya, Delacroix was fully conscious of his position as the heir to a long and rich tradition. While his works were full of references to his artistic, literary and musical heritage, however, they were also the innovative products of a personal vision and a passionate temperament. In his handling of colour, Delacroix was a greater influence on the Impressionists than anyone else, although their direct precursors were the painters of the Barbizon School, including Jean-Baptiste Camille Corot, Gustave Courbet and Narcisse Diaz de la Peña.

Inspired by seventeenth-century Dutch painting and early nineteenth-century English painting, the Barbizon painters sought with a new rigour to represent landscape as it was, unadulterated and unglamourised. Their honesty and realism influenced not only the French Impressionists but many other artists, including van Gogh and Liebermann, and it transformed representation of the landscape and its inhabitants, as in the work of van Gogh and Jean-François Millet. While Millet glorified peasants as heroes, the painter and caricaturist Honoré Daumier mirrored social conditions in a sharper, more disagreeable focus. The two paintings in the Gallery by Daumier are among his most famous. Auguste Rodin's work is also exhibited in other rooms, but this section houses his *Man with a broken nose* (plate 55), a masterpiece and metaphorical self-portrait that also recalls the classical heads of Greek philosophers, and for which the actual sitter was a worker in the Paris horse market. Its realism and resonance demonstrate Rodin's exceptional range and power, which is much greater than the term 'Impressionism' in its usual sense suggests.

Honoré Daumier, detail of *The play* (plate 50)

45

46

45

Théodore Géricault

Rouen 1791–1824 Paris

Bringing artillery to bear, c. 1814

Canvas, 89.2 × 143.7 cm

Inv. no. 8583

Acquired in 1910 on the Berlin art market

46

Théodore Géricault

Rouen 1791–1824 Paris

Heroic landscape with fishermen, 1818

Signed

Canvas, 249.5 × 217.5 cm

Inv. no. 14561

Acquired in 1978 on the New York art market

The 'staged' character of this picture is explained by its original purpose as wall decoration. Géricault painted this and two companion pieces in 1818 for a room in the house of his friend Marceau at Villers-Cotterets, near Paris.

47

Eugène Delacroix

Charenton-Saint Maurice 1798–1863 Paris

Clorinde frees Olindo and Sophronia, c. 1853–56

Signed

Canvas, 101 × 82 cm

Inv. no. 13165

Acquired in 1962 from a private collection in London

This depicts a scene from the second canto of *Gerusalemme Liberata* by Torquato Tasso (1544–95), which has as its subject the conquest of Jerusalem during the First Crusade in 1099. In Tasso's poem the Christian woman, Sophronia, took a stolen picture of the Virgin from the Mosque at Jerusalem, and was condemned to the stake along with her lover, Olindo. The chivalrous Saracen woman Chlorinde freed the lovers and persuaded the Sultan to pardon them.

47

48

49

48
Eugène Delacroix
Charenton-Saint Maurice 1798–1863
Paris
The death of Valentin, c. 1830
Signed
Canvas, 32.5 × 24.3 cm
Inv. no 14248
Bequeathed in 1971 by Theodor and
Woty Werner

The painting depicts a scene from
Goethe's *Faust* I (lines 3712f), in
which Valentin, Gretchen's brother,
dies after the duel with Faust and
Mephisto. Delacroix had earlier
seen Retzsch's Faust illustrations,
but what most impressed him was
an opera production in London in
1825. As well as a number of oils, the
artist subsequently produced some
lithographs on the theme. These
were published in 1828 and Goethe
himself thought highly of them.

49
Eugène Delacroix
Charenton-Saint Maurice 1798–1863 Paris
The death of Ophelia, 1838
Signed
Canvas, 37.9 × 45.9 cm
Inv. no. 12764
Acquired in 1958 from a private
collection in Switzerland

Delacroix has depicted the death of
Ophelia in *Hamlet* (Act IV, Scene 7):

There is a willow grows aslant a brook,
That shows his hoar leaves in the glassy stream;
There, with fantastic garlands did she come,
Of crow-flowers, nettles, daisies, and long purples,
That liberal shepherds give a grosser name,
But our cold maids do dead men's fingers call them,
There, on the pendant boughs her coronet weeds
Clambering to hang, an envious sliver broke;
When down the weedy trophies, and herself,
Fell in the weeping brook. Her clothes spread wide,
And, mermaid-like, a while they bore her up:
Which time, she chanted snatches of old tunes;
As one uncapable of her own distress,
Or like a creature native and indued
Unto that element: but long it could not be,
Till that her garments, heavy with their drink,
Pulled the poor wretch from her melodious lay
To muddy death.

The artist depicted the same scene in two
other versions (now in Paris and Winterthur).
The *Hamlet* lithographs which he produced
between 1834–43 also show how important
Shakespeare was to Delacroix.

50

51

50
Honoré Daumier
Marseilles 1808–1879 Valmondois
The play, c. 1860
Signed
Canvas, 97.5 × 90.4 cm
Inv. no. 8697
Gift of Reichsrat Theodor Freiherr
von Cramer-Klett in 1913 as part of
the Tschudi donation

51
Honoré Daumier
Marseilles 1808–1879 Valmondois
Don Quixote, c. 1868
Signed
Canvas, 52.2 × 32.8 cm
Inv. no. 8698
Gift of Karl Sternheim in 1913 as
part of the Tschudi donation

Daumier depicted the hero of
Cervantes' novel in a number of
paintings produced from the early
1850s onwards. The work in Munich
is a preparatory study for the
painting now in Boston.

52
Gustave Courbet
Ornans 1819–1877 La Tour de Peilz
The lock at Optevoz, 1854(?)
Signed
Canvas, 63.6 × 84.5 cm
Inv. no. 8584
Acquired in 1910 on the Paris art
market

Courbet and Charles-François
Daubigny first painted in the
Optevoz region (Isère) in 1854.
Daubigny also depicted the same
scene in a number of pictures.

53
Gustave Courbet
Ornans 1819–1877 La Tour de Peilz
Still life with apples, 1871
Signed
Canvas, 50.4 × 63.4 cm
Inv. no. 8623
Gift of M. von Nemes in 1911

Courbet produced this picture in
Ste-Pélagie prison, where he was
serving a sentence for his part in the
destruction of the Column in the
Place Vendome, Paris.

52

53

54

54
Jean-Baptiste Camille Corot
Paris 1796–1875 Paris
The bridge and the mill in Mantes
('Mantes – l'entrée du pont') *c.* 1860
Signed
Canvas, 25.5 × 33 cm
Inv. no. 8844
Acquired in 1915 on the Munich art
market

After 1855, Corot made frequent
visits to Mantes, north-west of
Paris, where he painted a number of
pictures.

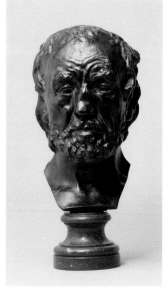

55

55
Auguste Rodin
Paris 1840–1917 Meudon
Man with a broken nose ('L' homme
au nez cassé'), 1863
Bronze, 30.5 cm high
Inv. no. L.209
Acquired in 1986 for the Bayerische
Versicherungskammer, Munich

In this head, Rodin combined the
ancient poet and philosopher bust-
type with realistic study from life,
and he also referred to Daniele da
Volterra's portrait of Michelangelo.
This early cast may have come from
the collection of the poet Robert
Browning.

56

56
Jean-François Millet
Gruchy 1814–1875 Barbizon
Grafting ('Le Greffeur'), 1855
Signed
Canvas, 80.5 × 100 cm
Inv. no. 14556
Acquired in 1978 on the New York
art market

In this picture, the analogy between
the new growth and the small child
is part of the symbolism that
characterises Millet, and which
made a deep impression on Vincent
van Gogh, whose painting in
general was greatly influenced by
Millet.

Late Romanticism and Realism in Germany

Three very important 'schools' of German painting in the nineteenth century are represented in this section: Berlin, Düsseldorf and Munich. The leading figure was Adolph von Menzel, one of the greatest German artists of the whole period, who spent most of his long career in Berlin. Menzel's distinctive graphic gifts and narrative skill found early expression in his illustrations for Kugler's *History of Frederick the Great* (1839–42), and numerous subsequent paintings reflect Menzel's virtual obsession with Prussia's age of glory, which only increased after the establishment of the Second Reich in 1871. Menzel represented scenes from the period with considerable subtlety. He usually avoided the general fashion for military heroics, preferring social scenes and occasions, which he liked to enliven with anecdotal touches. He was always interested in the human and psychological side of history, and his enormous output also includes scenes of contemporary life that depic virtually everything he might have encountered in the course of his own life. His works in this vein reveal not simply powers of observation but a surprisingly poetic eye; they are not mere literal representations. This is an aspect of his work that emerges most clearly in the sketches he made early in his career, during the 1840s, which were not intended for sale. These have an intensity and immediacy that is missing from the highly-detailed raconteur paintings of his later years.

Carl Spitzweg in Munich shared Menzel's penchant for anecdotal narrative, but in contrast his work has a sprinkling of mild irony that verges on caricature. Nevertheless, Spitzweg and his circle – Eduard Schleich, Dietrich Langko, Friedrich Voltz, Bernhard Stange and Christian Morgenstern – were progressive artists who, especially in their landscapes, reoriented their art towards the guiding principle of truth to nature and who were abreast, therefore, with the latest trends in France (the Barbizon School) and England (Constable, Turner).

Three of the best-known artists in the Düsseldorf 'school' are exhibited: Johann Wilhelm Schirmer and his pupils Andreas and Oswald Achenbach. Düsseldorf being so close to Holland, its artists were strongly influenced by Dutch art, especially the dramatic nature studies of Jacob van Ruisdael and Allaert van Everdingen. Thus, in their own way, these artists, participated in the general realist trend, which soon brought them considerable recognition.

Carl Spitzweg, detail of *The penniless poet* (plate 61)

57

58

57
Eduard Schleich the Elder
Haarbach 1812–1874 Munich
Landscape with withered oak, 1832
Signed and dated
Canvas, 60.3 × 75.5 cm
Inv. no. 8544
Acquired in 1908 on the Munich art market

This is the earliest known painting by Schleich.

58
Eduard Schleich the Elder
Haarbach 1812–1874 Munich
At Brannenburg, c. 1850
Signed
Panel, 30 × 38.7 cm
Inv. no. 8023
Bequeathed by the painter Anton Höchl in 1897

The castle and village of Brannenburg lie north-west of Falkenstein on the River Inn.

59
Johann Wilhelm Schirmer
Jülich 1807–1863 Karlsruhe
Stormy evening, c. 1860
Canvas, 38 × 60.5 cm
Inv. no. 9006
Acquired in 1919 from the
Heinemann Gallery, Munich

This painting may have been
inspired by impressions of the
Roman Campagna experienced by
Schirmer some twenty years earlier.

60
Carl Spitzweg
Munich 1808–1885 Munich
The nature walk, 1872
Signed
Canvas, 32.1 × 54.1 cm
Inv. no. 11995
Transferred from State ownership
in 1957

61
Carl Spitzweg
Munich 1808–1885 Munich
The penniless poet, 1839
Signed and dated
Canvas, 36.2 × 44.6 cm
Inv. no. 7751
Gift of Eugen Spitzweg in 1887

There is a second version of the
painting, very similar to this,
produced in the same year. In both
pictures, Spitzweg depicts, with
ironic humour, a poet who is
condemned to failure by the
inadequacy of his talents.

59

60

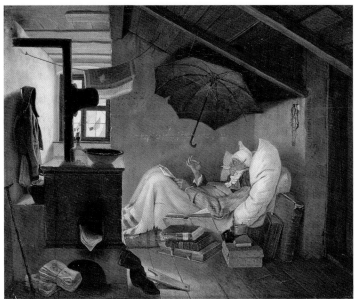

61

62

63

62

Andreas Achenbach
Kassel 1815–1910 Düsseldorf
Landscape with rune-stone, 1841
Signed and dated
Canvas, 34.5 × 52 cm
Inv. no. 14599
Gift of the Allianz-Versicherungs
AG, Munich, in 1979

Although painted on Mount Eifel in
western Germany, this landscape
probably reflects the artist's
impressions of Norway. The style is
reminiscent of the early German
Romantics, even though Achenbach
was a more realistic painter.

63

Oswald Achenbach
Düsseldorf 1827–1905 Düsseldorf
An Italian park, c. 1860
Signed
Canvas, 130.3 × 116.3 cm
Inv. no. 12512
Transferred from State ownership
in 1957

In this painting, Oswald
Achenbach, brother of Andreas,
uses motifs similar to those found
in pictures by Karl Blechen
(1798–1840).

64

Adolph von Menzel
Breslau 1815–1905 Berlin
*Living room with the
artist's sister*, 1847
Signed and dated
Paper, 46.1 × 31.6 cm
Inv. no. 8499
Acquired in 1937 from the artist's
niece, Margarethe Krigar-Menzel

The girl in the picture is Menzel's
younger sister, Emilie (born 1823),
with whom the artist had an
especially close relationship. After
his sister's marriage in 1859 to the
Director of the Royal Music,
Hermann Krigar, the couple set
up a common household with
Menzel, who was unmarried. In
the background, Menzel's mother
is at her sewing. Neither this nor
other similar early pictures made
as sketches were intended for
exhibition.

65

66

65
Adolph von Menzel
Breslau 1815–1905 Berlin
Private concert, 1851
Signed and dated
Gouache and pastel on paper,
mounted on panel, 44.7 × 58.9 cm
Inv. no. 8501
Acquired in 1937 from the artist's
niece, Margarethe Krigar-Menzel

66
Adolph von Menzel
Breslau 1815–1905 Berlin
In the railway carriage compartment,
c. 1848
Canvas, 43.1 × 52.2 cm
Inv. no. 9880
Acquired in 1912 on the Munich art
market

67

67
Adolph von Menzel
Breslau 1815–1905 Berlin
A procession in Hofgastein, 1880
Signed and dated
Canvas, 51.3 × 70.2 cm
Inv. no. L.817
On loan from the Federal Republic
of Germany since 1966

During the 1870s and 1880s, Menzel
often spent the summer in (Bad)
Hofgastein.

68
Adolph von Menzel
Breslau 1815–1905 Berlin
View from the Berliner Schloss, 1863
Signed and dated
Canvas, 52.6 × 37 cm
Inv. no. 8502.
Acquired in 1937 from the artist's
niece, Margarethe Krigar-Menzel

68

History Painting and Establishment Art

This section contains for the most part works of so-called 'official' art, that is art created by members and professors of the academies from the second half of the nineteenth century. It also contains work by independent artists, such as Franz von Lenbach and Albert von Keller, whose work similarly satisfied the expectations and needs of the establishment. Such works served the purpose of 'Repräsentation' or status enhancement. Many were public, that is 'history' paintings or sculpture intended for display within palaces, government buildings, churches, museums and so forth. In practice, the privately commissioned works on display in this section, the majority of which are individual and group portraits, had a semi-public function. These works were invariably painted in a historicist manner, echoing the Italian Renaissance, Flemish Baroque and later Dutch painting, thereby fulfilling the two main requirements of grandeur and monumentality.

During this period, and not only in Munich, a clear divide appeared between two kinds of art: that of the establishment and another kind of art that was committed to nature, for which there was little or no official outlet. On one side stood artists such as Wilhelm and Friedrich August von Kaulbach, Karl Theodor von Piloty, Hans Makart, Keller and Lenbach, and on the other side were men such as Leibl and his friends Marées and, early in his career, Liebermann. This was a new development, but it was connected to enormous social changes that were initiated in the late eighteenth century. A universal standard by which art could be assessed and judged no longer existed, and different criteria and values prevailed in different quarters.

In the Munich Academy, under the directorships of Cornelius (1824–40), Kaulbach (1849–74) and Piloty (1874–86), the absolute dominance of 'history' painting over genre, portrait, landscape and still-life painting was never called in to question. These artists felt themselves to be a part of the Renaissance tradition, and their employers, who were pillars of the State and the Church, saw themselves as successors to the patrons of Raphael, Titian, Rubens or van Dyck. In keeping with that tradition, they viewed 'history' painting not merely as decoration on a grand scale but as the representation of subjects with contemporary relevance, especially

Wilhelm von Kaulbach, detail of *The destruction of Jerusalem by the Emperor Titus* (plate 70)

those subjects that were significant in terms of national identity. In Munich, the grand tradition came to an end with Piloty's pupil Franz von Defregger, whose few 'history' paintings were dominated by a form of genre that had long been popular in Munich. Thus, this section also contains Defregger's sentimental genre pieces, Keller's elegant society gatherings and aristocratic portraits by Keller, Lenbach and Friedrich August von Kaulbach. In the last third of the nineteenth century literal and naturalistic realism became acceptable in official art, hence the works displayed here by Eduard Schleich, Adolf Lier, Dietrich Langko and Joseph Wenglein. These men, although not involved in the Academy, had a considerable following that included Leibl and his circle.

69

69
Wilhelm von Kaulbach
Arolsen 1804–1874 Munich
Ludwig I, surrounded by artists and scholars, descends from the throne to view the works of sculpture and painting presented to him, 1848
Signed and dated
Canvas 78.5 × 163 cm
Inv. no. WAF 406
Acquired by Ludwig I

Along with 18 other drafts, this picture is part of a cycle of preparatory works for frescoes on the exterior of the former Neue Pinakothek. The drafts were painted between 1848 and 1854. The frescoes themselves were executed by Christoph Nilson between 1850

and 1854. The theme laid down in the contract by Ludwig I was, '... recent developments in the Arts, called into being by *His Majesty the King*, and emanating from Munich'. It was intended that the drafts would be hung inside the Neue Pinakothek.

This draft for the middle section of the south wall shows Ludwig I as art collector against a background of the Glyptothek (centre), Alte Pinakothek (left) and State Library. The King's two principal areas of interest, Classical and Medieval art, are both represented.

70

70

Wilhelm von Kaulbach

Arolsen 1804–1874 Munich

*The destruction of Jerusalem by the
Emperor Titus*, 1846

Canvas, 585 × 705 cm

Dated

Inv. no. WAF 403

Acquired from the artist in 1846

Kaulbach's historical picture is full
of allegorical meaning, turning the
destruction of Jerusalem in AD 70
into a complex religio-historical
event, and its anti-Semitic content
is strongly in evidence. In the
artist's own opinion, he had
depicted a 'judgement which God
intended and carried out', as
described by Kaulbach in a detailed
printed commentary attached to his
picture. The great Prophets and the
seven Angels are shown at the top
of the picture. In the right-hand
background are the Emperor Titus
and his troops. In the middle
foreground the High Priest takes
his own life. In the left-hand
foreground the Eternal Jew is
pursued by demons, and, in
contrast, on the opposite side a
group of Christians (embodying the
Nazarenes' ideal of beauty) escape
destruction. Ludwig I, who
stipulated the dimensions of this
enormous painting, considered it
the most important picture in the
former Neue Pinakothek. As a key
work, purchased for the exceptional
sum of 35,000 guilders, it partly
determined the design of the
building and the layout of the
collection. Due to Kaulbach's
producing a commentary and
reproductions of his picture, it
became widely known during
his lifetime.

71

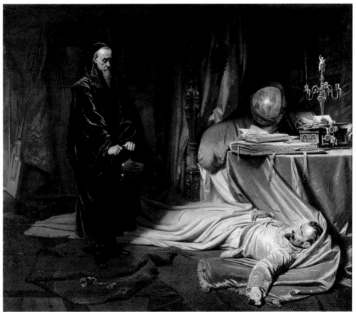

72

71

Karl Theodor von Piloty
Munich 1826–1886 Ambach
Thusnelda led in Germanicus's Triumph, 1869-73
Signed
Canvas, 490 x 710cm
Inv. no. WAF 771
Acquired from the artist in 1874

The subject matter comes from the *Annals* of Tacitus and from Strabo, reporting the campaigns of the Romans in Germany in the early first century AD. Thusnelda, wife of the German leader Arminius and daughter of the pro-Roman chieftain Segestes had been betrayed by her father and handed over to the Romans. With her son, Thumelicus, she was one of the prisoners in the triumph Germanicus held in Rome in AD 17. In the picture, on the tribune sits the emperor Tiberius, with Segestes on his right. Germanicus is in front of the triumphal arch. Like his German contemporaries, the artist saw the story in its wider implications as a confrontation between things German and things Roman, a confrontation which at the time of the Franco-Prussian War had assumed special relevance.

72

Karl Theodor von Piloty
Munich 1826–1886 Ambach
Seni before the body of Wallenstein, 1855
Canvas, 312 × 364.5 cm
Inv. no. WAF 770
Acquired from the artist by Ludwig I in 1855

The subject matter is taken from Schiller's *Wallenstein,* in particular Wallenstein's death (Act V, Scene 10), although the action happens off-stage. The artist combined several incidents within one powerful picture, suggesting an approaching disaster, which the astrologer reads in the stars. The painting established Piloty's reputation, and, from then on, he became one of the most celebrated European 'history' painters of his time.

73

74

73
Franz von Lenbach
Schrobenhausen 1836–1904 Munich
A Russian princess, 1863
Signed and dated
Canvas, 83.3 × 67.4 cm
Inv. no. 8873
Acquired in 1916 from the
Heinemann Gallery, Munich

The subject may be Maria
Nikolayevna, Countess Stroganov
(born 1819), Grand Duchess of
Russia by birth, and Dowager
Duchess of Leuchtenberg.

74
Franz von Defregger
Stronach 1835–1921 Munich
The last reserves, 1872
Signed and dated
Canvas, 53.4 × 70.2 cm
Inv. no. 9030
Acquired 1921 from the artist's estate

This sketch for a painting executed
in 1874 (now in Vienna) depicts the
last phase, in 1809, of the Tyrolean
War of Independence against
French occupation. A second very
similar sketch is also in the Bavarian
State art collections.

75

75
Albert-Ernest Carrier-Belleuse
Anizy-le-Château 1824–1887 Sèvres
Female Bust (*Flora*)
Marble, height 60.2 cm
Inv. no. B. 777
Acquired in 1981 from the Grünwald
Gallery, Munich

76
Albert von Keller
Gais 1844–1920 Munich
Chopin, 1873
Signed and dated
Panel, 85 × 69 cm
Inv. no. 8366
Gift of the art dealer August
Humpelmayr in 1905

Keller was especially fond of music,
and it frequently inspired his work:
'Visual ideas spontaneously spring
from acoustic stimuli'. This
painting established the artist's
reputation.

77
Hans Makart
Salzburg 1840–1884 Vienna
The falconer, c. 1880
Signed
Canvas, 106.3 × 79.9 cm
Inv. no. 12191
Transferred from State ownership
in 1962

76

77

German Artists in Rome

HANS VON MARÉES

Like several progressive artists of the second half of the nineteenth century, such as Cézanne and van Gogh, Hans von Marées received little or no recognition throughout most of his career. It is true that early on he achieved a degree of popularity and patronage for his portraits and pictures of horses, but for the figures he began painting around 1863 he received virtually none. He was dissatisfied with both of the prevailing standards: first, the official 'history' painting and the society pictures of Piloty, Keller and Lenbach; second, the 'truth to nature' school that was finally gaining acceptance as 'contemporary art'. Ironically, Marées had points in common with both; he derived his elevated subjects from the former, but found the way in which they were treated artificial, and from the Barbizon School and the 'moderns' he took a commitment to realism, while deploring the poverty of their subject matter.

In the early 1860s, while still living in Munich, Marées turned back to the Old Masters: at first to Rembrandt (chiefly his portraits); then to Titian, Raphael and Rubens; lastly to classical art. After finally settling in Rome in 1875 he devoted himself increasingly to large-scale figure compositions that represented Greek mythological subjects, biblical stories or subjects entirely of his own invention. He portrayed human beings simply as they were, stripped of all fleeting and circumstantial trappings, figures to be read as solitaries, couples or families and as Parting, Courtship, Love, Struggle or Death. Although he deliberately re-affirmed his connection with the Western artistic tradition, notably in his use of a sombre palette, the way in which Marées created timeless symbols or allegories of human life, and the technique with which he painted them, were both entirely modern. After his death Marées had an enormous influence on German artists.

The Gallery's considerable holdings of Marées' work come, with few exceptions, from the Conrad Fiedler Gift of 1891.

Anselm Feuerbach, detail of *Nanna* (plate 90)

78

79

78
Hans von Marées
Elberfeld (Wuppertal) 1837–1887
Rome
Self-portrait, 1883
Panel, 99.5 × 64 cm
Inv. no. 7868
Gift of Conrad Fiedler in 1891

Marées produced this self-portrait
for an exhibition of his work
planned for Berlin in 1883, which in
the end did not take place: 'To give
the pictures a certain credibility as
products of our age, I included a
life-size half-figure self-portrait.'

79
Hans von Marées
Elberfeld (Wuppertal) 1837–1887
Rome
The artist and Franz von Lenbach, 1863
Canvas, 54.3 × 62 cm
Inv. no. 7874
Gift of Conrad Fiedler in 1892

Shortly after Marées came to Munich
in 1857, he met Franz von Lenbach
(1836–1904), who later helped him
secure a commission from Adolf
Friedrich, Baron von Schack, to copy
works of the Old Masters in Italy. In
1878 Marées recalled his years in
Munich with Lenbach: '... In those
days that artistic dancing-bear was
not without influence on my life.'
In this painting, Lenbach is in the
foreground, with Marées behind him.

80
Hans von Marées
Elberfeld (Wuppertal) 1837–1887 Rome
Horsetamer and nymph, 1882–83
Panel, 188.5 × 144.5 cm
Inv. no. 7862
Gift of Conrad Fiedler in 1891

The picture is unfinished, and in
many places it reveals Marées'
characteristic use of tempera,
which he generally, if not
invariably, employed in the under-
painting.

80

81

82

81

Hans von Marées
Elberfeld (Wuppertal) 1837–1887
Rome
St George, 1885–87
Right wing of the triptych *The Three
Knights*, which represents *St Hubert*
in the centre and *St Martin* on the
left wing
Canvas, 183 × 117 cm
Inv. no. 7858
Gift of Conrad Fiedler in 1891

This triptych, including a painted
pedestal depicting the putti, was the
second version of a theme first
painted by Marées in 1880–81. Of his
first version, only the right-hand
panel has survived.

82

Hans von Marées
Elberfeld (Wuppertal) 1837–1887
Rome
Diana's rest, 1863
Canvas, 96.2 × 136 cm
Inv. no. 7866
Gift of Conrad Fiedler in 1891

Diana was identified with the
Greek goddess Artemis; she was
the virgin goddess of plants, game
and hunting; she was also the
protectress of women, and in art
she is often depicted with a female
retinue. In this painting, in
particular its use of colour, Marées
was inspired by Venetian painters,
especially Titian, although he had
yet to visit Italy.

83

83
Hans von Marées
Elberfeld (Wuppertal) 1837–1887
Rome
The Hesperides, 1884–85
Triptych of wooden panels, middle
panel 175.5 × 205 cm and each wing
175 × 88.5 cm
Inv. no. 7854
Gift of Conrad Fiedler in 1891

According to ancient mythology,
the Hesperides were nymphs who
tended the golden apples and fruit
trees in the divine Garden that lay
beyond the River Ocean. A tree with
golden fruit is a symbol either of
eternal youth or of love and
fertility. Accordingly Marées gave
the Hesperides a central position in
his picture of life's cycle.

84

84
Adolf von Hildebrand
Marburg 1847–1921 Munich
Conrad Fiedler, 1874–75
Marble, 44 cm high
Inv. no. B.295
Acquired in 1952 from Werner
Teupser

Conrad Adolf Fiedler (1841–95) had a
legal training, but because of his
considerable fortune he did not
need regular employment. He was
friendly with a number of artists,
including Adolf von Hildebrand,
Anselm Feuerbach and Hans von
Marées. He extended generous
financial support to Marées from
1868 until the artist's death. In 1891
Fiedler gave many works by Marées
to the Bavarian State art collections,
and these are now housed in the
Neue Pinakothek. Fiedler was also
an important art theorist.

BÖCKLIN, FEUERBACH, THOMA

At a time when the work of French artists was increasing in influence, first with the landscapes of the Barbizon School, Corot, Courbet, Théodore Rousseau and others, and then with the early Impressionism of Manet, Monet and Renoir, certain German painters, including Marées, Arnold Böcklin and Anselm Feuerbach, were drawn instead to Italy. They found in the countryside, art, culture and everyday life of Italy a world more satisfying than their own in Germany. For them, Italy evoked antiquity, which was their inspiration and, to a large degree, the source of their subject matter.

Feuerbach and Böcklin were temperamentally very different. Böcklin was nature-loving and his art is always sensuous, while Feuerbach's pictures are more introspective and intellectual. His *Medea* (plate 89) for example, is an ambitious and monumental statement, but lacks the human immediacy of Böcklin's *Pan amongst the reeds*, which engages not only the viewer's mind but also his empathy. For Böcklin *Stimmung*, or mood, was all-important, figures bringing out the mood of the landscape and the landscape reflecting the figures' feelings. In his earlier work, including *Pan amongst the reeds*, the *Stimmung* is less insistent; later he intensified it through every possible means, as in his burlesque *In the play of the waves*. This later painting is typical of Böcklin and far removed from Feuerbach, both in its humour and its palpable eroticism. Although both painters drew heavily on the Bible and mythology, Böcklin invented his own subject matter much more frequently than Feuerbach. Several of Böcklin's invented subjects are important examples of a trend that was both new and widespread in the last quarter of the nineteenth century: a trend towards imagery redolent with open-ended symbolism that is never declared or contextualised and may even be disturbingly enigmatic. Paintings such as *Villa by the sea* and *The Island of the Dead*, both of which exist in different versions, were of crucial importance for de Chirico and the Surrealists, while the surface decoration and tender yearning in other works, such as the *Ideal spring landscape*, anticipated Art Nouveau.

Hans Thoma travelled to Italy after studying with the landscape painter Johann Wilhelm Schirmer. *Memory of Orte*, 1887, captures his feelings towards Italy. A friend of Böcklin, who was twelve years his senior, Thoma also got to know Marées while staying there. Thoma was also influenced by Courbet and the Leibl circle, which can be seen in his closely observed *Landscape on the River Main* (plate 87), 1875, and his *Taunus landscape* (plate 88) of 1890. In the later painting, the wanderer shown resting and gazing into the distance is a motif clearly derived from earlier Romantic painters, such as Schwind and Friedrich.

85

Arnold Böcklin

Basel 1827–1901 Fiesole
In the play of the waves, 1883
Signed
Canvas, 180.3 × 237.5 cm
Inv. no. 7754
Gift of Jan Baron Wendelstadt of
Schloss Neubeuern

This picture is based on
impressions of the family of marine
zoologist Anton Dohrn as they
bathed together in the Gulf of
Naples. Böcklin introduced a
mythological dimension that
transformed the reality, with
comedic effect.

85

86

Arnold Böcklin

Basel 1827–1901 Fiesole
Pan amongst the reeds, 1859
Canvas, 199.7 × 152.6 cm
Inv. no. WAF 67
Acquired in 1859 by Ludwig I

Pan, the Greek god of flocks and
woods, is shown according to Ovid
(*Metamorphoses* I, 698f). Pan tried to
rape the nymph Syrinx, but she was
able to transform herself into reeds.
Pan made the reeds into pipes (pan
pipes), and Böcklin shows him
playing a lament for the vanished
Syrinx. Ludwig I purchased the
picture as soon as Böcklin had
completed it, thereby establishing
the artist's reputation.

86

87

88

87
Hans Thoma
Bernau (Black Forest) 1839–1924
Karlsruhe
Landscape on the River Main, 1875
Signed and dated
Canvas, 85.5 × 124.5 cm
Inv. no. 8878
Acquired in 1916 on the Munich art
market

88
Hans Thoma
Bernau (Black Forest) 1839–1924
Karlsruhe
Taunus landscape, 1890
Signed and dated
Canvas, 113.2 × 88.8 cm
Inv. no. 7834
Acquired in 1891 at the international
art exhibition in the Glaspalast,
Munich

89
Anselm Feuerbach
Speyer 1829–1880 Venice
Medea, 1870
Signed and dated
Canvas, 197 × 395 cm
Inv. no. 9826
Acquired by Ludwig II and in State
ownership since 1932

The sorceress Medea, daughter of
King Aietes of Colchis, helped Jason
of the Argonauts in his quest for the
Golden Fleece. She had two sons by
Jason, whom she murdered when
he left her. A performance of Ernest
Legouvé's play *Medea* in Rome in
1866, with Adelaide Ristori in the
title role, kindled Feuerbach's
obsession with the subject, which
he painted several times.

89

90

90
Anselm Feuerbach
Speyer 1829–1880 Venice
Nanna, 1861
Signed
Canvas, 137.8 × 99.3 cm
Inv. no. 9610
Acquired in 1930 on the Munich art
market

In 1860 Feuerbach became
interested in Nanna Risi, a working-
class Roman who reminded him of
Raphael's Madonnas. In the same
year Nanna left her husband and
children to live with the artist,
staying with him for five years.
During this time the artist executed
several portraits of her and used her
as a model for several of his
historical figures.

Wilhelm Leibl and his Circle

While he was studying at the Munich Academy, from 1864 to 1869, Wilhelm Leibl was the dominant personality within a circle of artists, the original nucleus of which included Johann Sperl, Theodor Alt, Rudolf Hirth du Frênes and Fritz Schider. They were joined in the early 1870s by Wilhelm Trübner, Carl Schuch and several others. Leibl and his friends were committed to the principle of 'truth to nature'. In particular, Leibl and Schuch favoured figures, landscapes, domestic scenes and still lifes, which they portrayed faithfully but not unimaginatively according to their direct experience. They received stimulus and support from artists of an earlier generation, such as Schleich, Lier and Langko, who worked in Munich outside the Academy and had contact with members of the Barbizon School. They also drew inspiration from seventeenth-century Dutch landscape and genre painting and from the admiration for such art that had been growing since Georges Michel revived French interest early in the nineteenth century. For the Leibl circle, Dutch painting was 'modern'; as ordinary citizens' art, it conformed well with their ideal. In his 1869 portrait *Frau Gedon*, Leibl borrowed quite obviously from Rembrandt's *Jan Six*. His picture aroused considerable interest at the Internationale Kunstausstellung (International Art Exhibition) in Munich of that year, bringing Leibl the friendship of Courbet and an invitation to Paris, where the young German was no less successful.

Courbet and the Barbizon School exerted a direct influence on these artists. In *Kähnsdorf Lock* Schuch introduced a motif from Courbet's painting, and time and again in his later landscapes Schuch took up ideas found in the work of the French painter. Further developments in French art had an impact, and Manet's influence is visible in Leibl's portrait *Lina Kirchdorffer*, completed shortly after his return from Paris, and in still lifes by Schuch, who lived in Paris from 1882 to 1894.

Other artists in the circle were less rigorous in their adherence to truth and experience. For example, Sperl tended towards the sentimental and anecdotal, never eliminating it entirely from his work, while Trübner's later output was generally uninspired, though his *In the studio* (plate 93) of 1872 is one of the finest pictures produced by the Leibl circle.

Wilhelm Leibl, detail of *Lina Kirchdorffer* (plate 94)

The only recognition that Leibl and his friends received during their lifetimes was the admiration of a small circle of other artists and connoisseurs. While Lenbach was celebrated throughout Europe, building himself a villa in Munich in the style of the Italian Renaissance, Leibl grew disgusted by the art market and moved to the country in 1873.

91

91

Wilhelm Leibl
Cologne 1844–1900 Würzburg
The painter Jean Paul Selinger,
c. 1880
Signed
Canvas, 45 × 37 cm
Inv. no. 8264
Acquired in 1903 on the Munich art market

Selinger (1850–1909) came to Munich in the mid-1870s, and there, with fellow Americans Frank Duveneck, William Merrit Chase and J. Frank Currier, he joined Wilhelm Leibl's circle. He returned to the USA in 1881 and settled in Providence, Rhode Island.

92

Wilhelm Leibl
Cologne 1844–1900 Würzburg
Mina Gedon, 1868–69
Canvas, 119.5 × 95.7 cm
Inv. no. 8708
Acquired on the Munich art market

Mina Gedon, the young wife of the Munich architect Lorenz Gedon, did many tiring sittings for Leibl while she was pregnant. Leibl scored great success with her portrait at exhibitions in Munich and Paris in 1869–70. It was artists, including Gustave Courbet, who were especially enthusiastic about the painting.

92

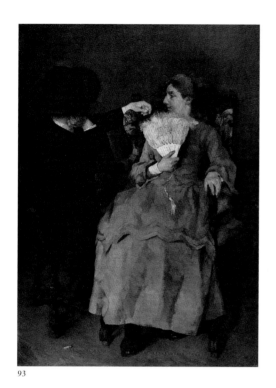

93

94

93
Wilhelm Trübner
Heidelberg 1851–1917 Karlsruhe
In the studio, 1872
Signed and dated
Canvas, 82 × 61 cm
Inv. no. 8108
Acquired in 1899 from the artist

94
Wilhelm Leibl
Cologne 1844–1900 Würzburg
Lina Kirchdorffer, 1871
Canvas, 111 × 83.5 cm
Inv. no. 8446
Acquired in 1907 on the Munich art market

Leibl produced this portrait of his niece Lina immediately after he returned from Paris. In his fluid sensitive brushwork, he shows the influence of Édouard Manet. Lina married the painter Fritz Schider in 1873.

95
Carl Schuch
Vienna 1846–1903 Vienna
Still life with apples, wine glass and tin jug, c. 1876
Signed with a facsimile stamp
Canvas, 69.5 × 92 cm
Inv. no. 8563
Acquired in 1909 at the Schuch retrospective held at the Kunstverein, Munich

This is one of the first still lifes ever painted by Schuch. There is a very similar version, painted the same year, in the Alte Nationalgalerie, Berlin.

96
Carl Schuch
Vienna 1846–1903 Vienna
Still life with asparagus, c. 1885–90
Signed with a facsimile stamp
Canvas, 79 × 63 cm
Inv. no. 8907
Acquired in 1916 at the auction of the Schmeil collection in Berlin

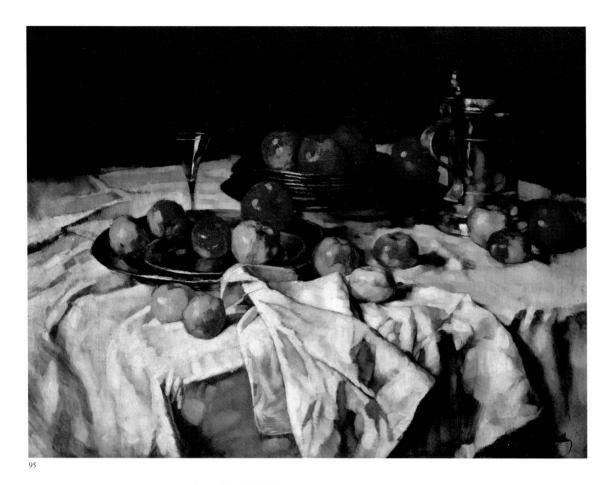

95

96

97

97
Carl Schuch
Vienna 1846–1903 Vienna
Rocky forest landscape, c. 1890
Signed (stamp)
Canvas, 62 × 83 cm
Inv. no. 8564
Acquired in 1909

This is a relatively late landscape by
the painter. Schuch painted it
around 1890 at the Saut du Doubs,
in the Jura northwest of Neuchâtel,
making a number of references to
Courbet.

98

98
Johann Sperl
Buch 1840–1914 Bad Aibling
The Kindergarten, c. 1884
Signed
Canvas, 71.3 × 101.6 cm
Inv. no. BGM 5
Acquired in 1984 for the collection
of the Bayerische Landesbank

French Impressionism

AND CÉZANNE, GAUGUIN, VAN GOGH

'Impressionism' means painting everyday life in the open air. The term was coined from a painting produced by Monet in 1872 entitled *Impression, soleil levant* (Sunrise: an impression), and it was applied to artists who participated in an exhibition at Nadar's Gallery in 1874, including Monet, Cézanne, Degas, Pissarro, Renoir and Sisley. These painters differed in style and approach very considerably. Moreover, Gauguin and van Gogh, who had little in common with Monet, Renoir or Sisley, both had 'Impressionist' phases.

While the art recognised and promoted by the academies was above all still 'history' painting, the Barbizon School and others who shared their views had turned instead to landscape and ordinary middle-class or peasant subjects, championing 'truth to nature' or experience. This was also the guiding principle of the Impressionists, who, stimulated partly by Constable and by Delacroix, found that it required lightening of the palette, avoiding the use of grey and ochre in shading, and use of unmixed luminous colours. They were led to employ a looser more spontaneous brushwork, with which, inevitably, they were unable to create the illusion of solidity and the distinctness of things. With flat dabs on the canvas, however, they achieved instead a homogeneous surface within which all was merged to a single effect. Sketchily painted in brilliant colours and unburdened by weighty significance, the landscapes, portraits and scenes of ordinary life that they painted from the early 1870s reflect the cheerful and carefree side of nature and life. There were, however, considerable differences between the work of Monet, Renoir and Sisley and that of Manet, Degas and Cézanne.

Before he became an Impressionist, Édouard Manet was the last great artist in the Western tradition with a feeling for the substance and texture of his subjects – flowers, glass, fabrics and people, who, in his work, are alive in flesh and spirit. Manet's human subjects have a distinct self-awareness, combining an outward elegance with a certain melancholy that one can believe was characteristic of the Parisian *haute bourgeoisie* of the second half of the nineteenth century. His painting

Breakfast in the studio, 1868, is a masterpiece of this early period and one of the finest he ever produced. Although he turned to Impressionism, or *plein-air* painting, in 1873–74, Manet's figures retained their distinctive portrait quality, whereas for Monet, Pissarro and Renoir figures had little importance or at least minimal characterisation.

Edgar Degas had much more in common with his friend Manet than with the other Impressionists. Degas portrayed figures with an even sharper and increasingly critical eye, as well as irony and sometimes even sarcasm, as in his numerous pictures of women bathing, which date from the second half of the 1880s. As they washed and dried themselves, Degas drew the women from unconventional angles, producing compositions that are obviously influenced by Japanese prints.

From this point in Degas' development Henri de Toulouse-Lautrec's picks up. Indeed, he is Degas taken to an extreme. Irony and wit are the dominant ingredients of his prints and posters. These elements are less pronounced in his early paintings influenced by Manet, but they emerge more strongly in drawings and oil studies of the theatre and brothels, which the artist began to produce during the second half of the 1880s.

Paul Cézanne abandoned his early sombre and intensely passionate style to take up Impressionism under the tutelage of Camille Pissarro, although he never followed the general tendency towards a free, flat and sketchy execution. In his landscapes, still lifes, portraits and figure compositions – in particular, his *Bathers* series – he gave his subjects weight and pregnancy by removing them from time and circumstance. With the waning of Neo-Impressionism and Art Nouveau, Cézanne became a seminal influence on the new Cubist movement.

Paul Gauguin and his circle, including Emile Bernard, Paul Sérusier and others, were the most important figures in the emergence of Art Nouveau. They were prompted, particularly by Japanese woodcuts, to explore the tendency within Impressionism towards two-dimensionality and decoration for its own sake. In addition, Gauguin liked to embrace mystical and universal themes, combining motifs from South Sea Islands culture with a basically Christian outlook, as in *The birth of Christ* (plate 120), 1896. He is therefore also an important figure within Symbolist art.

Schooled in the Old Masters, the Barbizon School and The Hague School, Delacroix and Impressionism, Vincent van Gogh was a distinct and isolated figure. In common with Gauguin, however, he dedicated himself to painting pictures that were of universal significance, encompassing all human joy and sorrow.

Nearly all the works in this section were donated between 1911 and 1913 by Munich citizens and some artists as a memorial to Hugo von Tschudi (1851–1911, Director of the Bayerische Staatsgemäldesammlungen from 1909 until his death).

99

99
Édouard Manet
Paris 1832–1883 Paris
Breakfast in the studio, 1868
Signed
Canvas, 118 × 154 cm
Inv. no. 8638
Given in 1911 by Georg Ernst von
Schmidt-Reissig as part of the
Tschudi donation

This picture combines the genres of
interior scene and portraiture. The
young man is Manet's illegitimate
son Léon Leenhoff-Koella, whose
mother, Suzanne Leenhoff, the
artist subsequently marrried.

100

101

100

Auguste Rodin
Paris 1840–1917 Meudon
Eve, 1885(?)
Terracotta, 72 cm high
Inv. no. B.355
Acquired in 1959 on the art market
in Switzerland

Rodin created the figure of Eve,
together with that of Adam, for his
Gates of Hell (about 1880–81), but he
did not retain the original design.
A 170 cm-high cast exists from this
early stage. Around 1885, Rodin
created a marble version 70 cm
high, which was followed by ten
further marble versions of *Eve*.
Judging by its size, this figure in
terracotta is related to the first
marble version.

101

Edgar Degas
Paris 1834–1917 Paris
Dancer, c. 1890–1900
Signed
Bronze, height 45 cm
Inv. no B. 134
Acquired 1929 on the Munich art
market

102

102
Pierre-Auguste Renoir
Limoges 1841–1919 Cagnes-sur-Mer
Young woman in a black blouse, 1876
Signed
Canvas, 60.5 × 40.5 cm
Inv. no. 8644
Given anonymously in 1912 as part
of the Tschudi donation

103

103

Claude Monet
Paris 1840–1926 Giverny
The bridge over the Seine at Argenteuil,
1874
Signed and dated
Canvas, 60 × 81.3 cm
Inv. no. 8642
Acquired in 1912 on the Berlin art
market

After the Franco-Prussian War
Monet lived for five years in
Argenteuil, as did Édouard Manet
and Alfred Sisley. The bridge shown
here was built in 1872.

104

104

Édouard Manet
Paris 1832–1883 Paris
The boat, 1874
Signed
Canvas, 82.5 × 105 cm
Inv. no. 8759
Acquired in 1914 as part of the
Tschudi donation

This work was painted in the year
of the first Impressionist
exhibition. It shows Claude Monet
with his wife on the artist's boat.
Monet painted several of his
pictures while on board his boat.
During that year, he and Manet had
a particularly close friendship.

105

106

105
Camille Pissarro
St-Thomas 1830–1903 Paris
A road in Upper Norwood, 1871
Signed
Canvas, 45.3 × 55.5 cm
Inv. no. 8699
Given in 1913 by L. Prager as part of
the Tschudi donation

Like Claude Monet and Alfred
Sisley, Pissarro moved to England
during the Franco-Prussian War.
Upper Norwood is a southern
suburb of London.

106
Alfred Sisley
Paris 1839–1899 Moret-sur-Loing
A Road in Hampton Court, 1874
Signed and dated
Canvas, 38.8 × 55.8 cm
Inv. no. 13134
Acquired in 1961 on the Paris art
market

The singer Jean-Baptiste Fauré
made it possible for Sisley to visit
England in 1874. He also collected
the artist's work.

107

108

107
Edgar Degas
Paris 1834–1917 Paris
Henri and Alexis Rouart, 1895
Signed
Canvas, 92 × 73 cm
Inv. no. 13681
Acquired in 1965 on the New York
art market

Henri Rouart (1833–1912), a friend of
Degas, was an engineer who also
painted and exhibited with the
Impressionists. He was also one of
the most important collectors of his
time. He is depicted with his son
Alexis. Preparatory drawings of
both subjects exist.

108
Edgar Degas
Paris 1834–1917 Paris
After bathing, c. 1888–92
Signed and inscribed 'A M J
Stchoukine'
Pastel on paper, 48 × 63 cm
Inv. no. 13136
Acquired on the London art market
in 1961

The inscription indicates that this
pastel was a gift from the artist to
the Russian merchant and well-
known collector, Sergei Ivanovich
Shtshukin, who had met Degas in
1908 and appreciated his work.

109
Edgar Degas
Paris 1834–1917 Paris
The ironer, c. 1869
Marked with the executor's stamp
Canvas, 92.5 × 74 cm
Inv. no. 14310
Acquired in 1972 on the New York
art market

The picture is unfinished. The
model was Emma Dobigny, whose
portrait Degas painted in 1869.

109

110

110
Paul Cézanne
Aix-en-Provence 1839–1906 Aix-en-
Provence
Self-portrait, c. 1875–77
Canvas, 55.5 × 46 cm
Inv. no. 8648
Given in 1912 by Eduard Arnhold
and Robert von Mendelssohn as
part of the Tschudi donation

111
Paul Cézanne
Aix-en-Provence 1839–1906 Aix-en-
Provence
Still life, c. 1885
Canvas, 73 × 92 cm
Inv. no. 8647
Acquired in 1912 as part of the
Tschudi donation

112
Paul Cézanne
Aix-en-Provence 1839–1906 Aix-en-
Provence
The railway cutting, c. 1870
Canvas, 80 × 129 cm
Inv. no. 8646
Acquired in 1912 as part of the
Tschudi donation

The railway cutting was not far
from the Jas de Bouffan, near Aix-
en-Provence in the Arc valley. In the
background is Cézanne 's first
depiction of Mont St-Victoire,
which was to be such a frequent
motif in his paintings in later years.

111

112

113

115

114

116

113
Henri de Toulouse-Lautrec
Albi 1864–1901 Malromé
A female portrait, 1897
Signed
Board, 63 × 48 cm
Inv. no. 8666
Given in 1912 by Eduard Arnhold
and Robert von Mendelssohn as
part of the Tschudi donation

114
Vincent van Gogh
Groot-Zundert 1853–1890 Auvers-
sur-Oise
The weaver, 1884
Canvas, 67.7 × 93.2 cm
Inv. no. 14249
Bequeathed in 1971 by Theodor and
Woty Werner

During his time in Nuenen
(1883–85), van Gogh produced
numerous drawings, watercolours
and oils of the weavers he met.

115
Henri de Toulouse-Lautrec
Albi 1864–1901 Malromé
The young Routy at Céleyran, 1882
Signed with a monogram stamp
Canvas, 61 × 49.8 cm
Inv. no. 14928
Acquired in 1984 with the aid of the
Ernst von Siemens art fund

Routy was a farm labourer, who
worked for the castle of Céleyran
near Narbonne. The castle belonged
to Toulouse-Lautrec's grandmother,
and the artist was a frequent visitor
in his early years. He painted the
castle and its estate from 1880
onwards. In 1882 he began a series of
works devoted to the young Routy.

116
Vincent van Gogh
Groot-Zundert 1853–1890 Auvers-
sur-Oise
The plain at Auvers, 1890
Canvas, 73.5 × 92 cm
Inv. no. 9584
Acquired in 1929 on the Paris art
market

The artist reached Auvers on 21 May
1890. From a letter dated 23 July that
had a sketch of this picture it can be
deduced that van Gogh had just
completed it.

117

118

117
Vincent van Gogh
Groot-Zundert 1853–1890 Auvers-
sur-Oise
Vase with sunflowers, 1888
Signed
Canvas, 91 × 72 cm
Inv. no. 8672
Given anonymously in 1912 as part
of the Tschudi donation

Van Gogh created this, and his other
pictures of sunflowers, to decorate
his house in Arles and the rooms of
his friends Paul Gauguin and Emile
Bernard, whose arrival he looked
forward to. Van Gogh also intended
the sunflower pictures to be the
side panels of a triptych with his
rocking chair (*La Berceuse*) in the
centre.

118
Vincent van Gogh
Groot-Zundert 1853–1890 Auvers-
sur-Oise
View of Arles, 1889
Canvas, 72 × 92 cm
Inv. no. 8671
Given in 1912 by Emy Roth as part of
the Tschudi donation

This is one of several views of Arles
that van Gogh produced after
moving there in 1888. In contrast to
other pictures, the restriction of the
view by poplar trees suggests that
the artist had abandoned hope of
creating an ideal community in
Arles. Van Gogh's feelings of
resignation were due to a mental
illness that led to his confinement
to the psychiatric institution at
St-Remy.

119

119
Paul Gauguin
Paris 1848–1903 Atuana
Four Breton women, 1886
Signed and dated
Canvas, 72 × 90 cm
Inv. no. 8701
Given in 1913 by Emy Roth as part of
the Tschudi donation

120
Paul Gauguin
Paris 1848–1903 Atuana
The Birth of Christ, 1896
Signed, dated and inscribed 'TE
TAMARI NO ATUA'
Canvas, 96 × 131 cm
Inv. no. 8652
Given in 1912 by Eduard Arnhold
and Robert von Mendelssohn as
part of the Tschudi donation

The inscription means 'Children of
God', although the artist probably
meant 'Child of God'. The picture
was painted to mark the birth of
a child, in 1896, to the Tahitian
woman Pajura, whom Gauguin
had taken as his wife. The child
died a few days later. Deliberate
references to Christian themes had
already appeared in the artist's
earlier work.

121
Auguste Rodin
Paris 1840–1917 Meudon
Crouching woman, 1880–82
Signed
Bronze, 85 cm high
Inv. no. B.58
Given anonymously as part of the
Tschudi donation

Several smaller versions in
terracotta and bronze preceded
this sculpture, for which Rodin
used his model Adèle. In the smaller
versions the woman is sometimes
accompanied by a male figure. In
1882 the pair were made into a
group entitled *Je suis belle*. Rodin
also intended to adapt the larger-
scale *Crouching woman* as a caryatid.

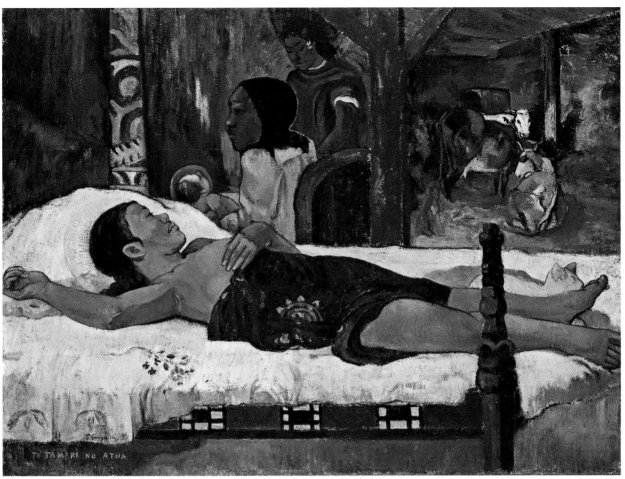

120

121

Social Realism and 'Plein-air' Painting

This section features work by Dutch and German artists, some of whom (Max Liebermann, Fritz von Uhde and Max Slevogt) were on the threshold of Impressionism. A key role was played by Liebermann, who, like his contemporary van Gogh, was committed to nature as the basis of art, looking for guidance to seventeenth-century Dutch painting and the Barbizon School. These consciously middle-class artists took as their model the unadorned citizens' art of Rembrandt, Frans Hals and the like. They were devoted to the portrayal of the simple folk, for the most part the peasantry, although they later extended their interest to the urban bourgeoisie and eventually the industrial working classes as well.

For the Germans, Millet and Jozef Israëls were the immediate predecessors, but, while he greatly appreciated their work, Liebermann did not follow its religious symbolism. Uhde gave the Christian message modern expression in a wide range of works, and Slevogt, who was a kindred spirit to writers such as Gerhart Hauptmann, made an unequivocal appeal to the spectator's social conscience in works such as *After work* (plate 126). However, in one of Liebermann's masterpieces – *Woman with goats among dunes* (plate 123) – it is difficult to find any social comment.

The Dutch artists represented in this section belonged to the so-called School of The Hague, a loosely connected group who, from about 1870 in The Hague and later elsewhere, stressed freshness and immediacy in their painting of nature. The 'School' spans two generations: painters born around 1830, such as Johannes Bosboom, Willem Roelofs, Jozef Israëls and Jan Hendrik Weissenbruch, and others born around 1840, including Paul Joseph Gabriel, the Maris brothers, Anton Mauve, Hendrik Willem Mesdag, Johannes Bilders, Bernardus Blommers and Albert Neuhuys. These painters were a formative influence on van Gogh, and were themselves formed by the native tradition of landscape painting and the work of the Barbizon School.

Max Liebermann was a complex and pivotal figure. His *Munich beer garden* was directly inspired by a similar picture by Menzel, and it is also clearly influenced by both the Dutch realist tradition and French Impressionism, particularly Édouard Manet's *Music in the Tuileries Gardens*, 1862. Uniting several trends, it is something of a landmark.

Max Liebermann, detail of *Munich Beer Garden* (plate 124)

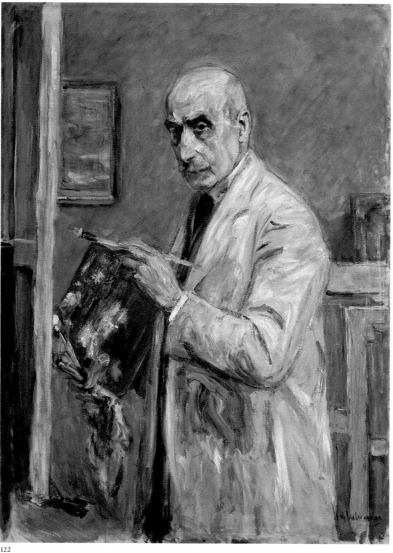

122

122
Max Liebermann
Berlin 1847–1935 Berlin
Self-portrait, c. 1922
Signed
Canvas, 113.5 × 85 cm
Inv. no. 12421
Acquired 1956

This is one of a large number of self-portraits by the artist, which were painted throughout his career. The subdued colour and the relaxed brushwork show the influence of Frans Hals.

123
Max Liebermann
Berlin 1847–1935 Berlin
A woman with goats among the dunes, 1890
Signed and dated
Canvas, 127 × 172 cm
Inv. no. 7815
Acquired from the artist in 1891

124
Max Liebermann
Berlin 1847–1935 Berlin
Munich beer garden, 1883–84
Signed
Panel, 94.5 × 68.5 cm
Inv. no. 14979
Acquired in 1986 with the aid of the Ernst von Siemens art fund

This painting was inspired by impressions of the Augustiner beer garden in Munich. Liebermann made numerous preparatory studies.

123

124

125

125
Jacob Maris
The Hague 1837–1899 Karlsbad
Dutch Landscape, 1890–91
Signed
Canvas, 85 × 134 cm
Inv. no. 7838
Acquired in 1891 at the international
art exhibition in the Glaspalast,
Munich

This work is the first of a group of
oil and watercolour landscapes, in
which the artist painted variations
of the towpath motif.

126
Max Slevogt
Landshut 1868–1932 Neukastel
After work, 1900–01
Signed
Canvas, 126 × 155 cm
Inv. no. 8181
Acquired in 1901 at the
international art exhibition in the
Glaspalast, Munich

Slevogt wrote of this picture: '. . .
And so I paint a couple, sitting
together. Whilst it is primarily an
exercise in painting, it should also
give free rein to darker emotions.
Her face is secretive, inscrutable.
His is turned towards her. If one
needs a meaning, it will be
something like this: even the
poorest people have a right to a
place at the table of life.'

127
Albert Neuhuys
Utrecht 1844–1914 Locarno
Spring, 1885(?)
Signed
Canvas, 38 × 50 cm
Inv. no. 7787
Purchased by the State in 1889

126

127

German Impressionism

The term 'Impressionist' says even less about the German artists it is used to describe than it does about the French artists who are grouped beneath it. The term is widely used to describe brightly coloured cheerful pictures, in which surface pattern prevails over traditional composition in terms of space and three-dimensional form. German artists seldom achieved the French brilliance of colour, however, because they were unwilling to abandon middle tones of brown, ochre and grey. They were influenced less by early Impressionism than by the work of van Gogh and later the Fauves, with their energetic brush strokes and glaring violent colours. At the same time the German artists had a greater tendency towards narrative elements, and in general they appealed as much to the heart and mind as to the eye. In Germany, artists such as Lovis Corinth or Max Slevogt did not abandon mythological and literary subjects for the French Impressionists' almost exclusive concentration on genre, still life and landscape.

Max Liebermann (born in 1847), Lovis Corinth and Max Slevogt (born respectively ten and 20 years later) are the three main figures in German Impressionism. In their search for a felt connection with nature, all were inspired by seventeenth-century Dutch painting, the Barbizon School and the French Impressionists, although Liebermann was a mediating influence on the other two. All three painted mostly portraits and landscapes, but Corinth was also drawn to mythological, biblical and historical subjects, and Slevogt worked within illustration and stage design (for productions of Goethe's *Faust* and Mozart's *Don Giovanni* and *The Magic Flute*), while Liebermann increasingly turned away from the narrative pictures of his earlier career. While these three men were Impressionists who associated more or less closely with other artists, such as Fritz von Uhde, they were very different, too. To summarise, Liebermann was realist and objective, Corinth was a spirited temperament but had wistful moments and Slevogt was imaginative, decorative and anecdotal.

Lovis Corinth, detail of *The fishermen's cemetery at Nidden* (plate 132)

128

128
Max Slevogt
Landshut 1868–1932 Neukastel
A sunny corner of the garden at
Neukastel, 1921
Signed and dated
Canvas, 90 × 100 cm
Inv. no. 9094
Acquired from the artist in 1922

Slevogt purchased the Neukastel
estate in the Palatinate shortly
before the First World War. It was
here that he met his wife.

129

129
Max Liebermann
Berlin 1847–1935 Berlin
Boys bathing, 1898
Signed and dated
Canvas, 122 × 151 cm
Inv. no. 14679
Given in 1980

Liebermann painted many versions
on this theme, and he also altered
this painting many times. The
picture draws on impressions of
Holland, which the artist visited
often.

130

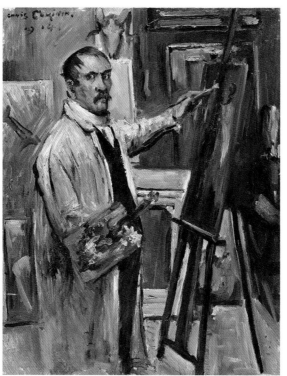

131

130

Lovis Corinth

Tapiau 1858–1925 Zandvoort

Eduard Graf von Keyserling, 1901

Signed and dated

Canvas, 99.5 × 75.5 cm

Inv. no. 8986

Acquired in 1919 on the Munich art market

Keyserling (1855–1918) was a short-story writer and dramatist, who suffered poor health from 1893 onwards. He was a friend of Frank Wedekind, Karl Kraus, Max Halbe and others.

131

Lovis Corinth

Tapiau 1858–1925 Zandvoort

Self-portrait at the easel, 1914

Signed and dated

Panel, 73 × 57.5 cm

Inv. no. 1189

Acquired in 1950 on the Munich art market

This shows the artist after suffering a stroke in 1911, which had caused his technique to change significantly.

132

Lovis Corinth

Tapiau 1858–1925 Zandvoort

The fishermen's cemetery at Nidden, 1893

Signed and dated

Canvas, 113 × 148 cm

Inv. no. 12043

Acquired in 1954 from the collection of Carl Nicolai

Nidden was an East Prussian fishing village and bathing resort on the Kurische Nehrung, which came under Soviet control in 1945.

132

International Art Around 1900

The last section of the Neue Pinakothek illustrates various trends from around the turn of the twentieth century, which immediately preceded Fauvism, Cubism, Die Brücke and Der Blaue Reiter. Although some of the works on display were made after the advent of these movements, only the two paintings by Albert Weisgerber reveal the influence of an artist such as Matisse.

From the French 'school', paintings by Claude Monet and Paul Signac exemplify the later phase of Impressionism and so-called Neo-Impressionism. In their flat decorative use of colour, the Nabis or 'Prophets' (Maurice Denis, Pierre Bonnard and Édouard Vuillard) were influenced most strongly by Gauguin. Maurice Denis and Odilon Redon adopted a symbolism that reflected to a varying extent their Christian belief.

Around 1900 a taste for unashamedly flat and highly decorative paintings prevailed throughout Europe. Known in Germany as *Jugendstil* and in France and in the English-speaking world as Art Nouveau, this style can be traced to the influence of Japanese art. Known in the West from about 1860, Japanese art prepared the way for the emergence of abstract art. Art Nouveau embraced all the arts, not least architecture, and its leading centres were London, Glasgow, Paris, Brussels, Munich and Vienna. Generally speaking, its most serious practitioners attempted to combine truth to nature with beauty of form, which was not viewed in terms of an historicist style.

Some artists, for instance Gustav Klimt in Vienna, transmuted forms into precious glittering decoration. Others, such as Vuillard in France and Edvard Munch in Norway, created spectacular and nightmarish shapes. To a greater or lesser degree, these artists wanted to express concepts of overwhelming importance, but they did not, alas, always communicate their ideas without descending into bathos or banality. Some artists handled the grand themes of love, death and religion quite casually, or as a means to erotic titillation, the classic example of which is Franz von Stuck's *Sin* (plate 144). Artists such as James Ensor,

133

133
Giovanni Segantini
Arco 1858–1899 Pontresina
Ploughing, 1887–90
Signed and dated
Canvas, 116 × 227 cm
Inv. no. 7997
Acquired in 1892, at the exhibition
of the Munich Sezession

This picture originally existed in a
different form, but was later
reworked by Segantini.

Egon Schiele and, in particular, Edvard Munch had more serious motivations, each different. Munch's imagery, combining the influence of van Gogh and Gauguin with Nordic motifs, is genuinely affecting, and it successfully conveys an impression of sinister and painful psychic forces from which there is no escape.

Particular attention should be paid to two sculptures, both made in Paris during the first decade of the twentieth century, although by artists from different generations. The *Portrait of Helene Nostitz* (plate 148) is characteristic of Rodin's later style, insofar as his conspicuously soft treatment of marble gives his work the character of combined dream and reality; on the one hand, the woman appears to be dreaming, and on the other, she appears to the viewer as his or her own dream image. This oscillation between reality and perception is typical of the broad current of Symbolism, to which Rodin made an essential contribution. The fine modelling and sensitive expression of Picasso's *The fool* (plate 147), another important piece of sculpture, show that this is one of the artist's early works, created at the same time as numerous pictures of harlequins during the artist's so-called Pink Period. The delicacy of characterisation is not pushed as far as the state of suspension found in Rodin's work. His encounter with the art of Cézanne, however, would soon lend Picasso's work expressive solidity.

Paul Signac, detail of *Maria della Salute* (plate 135)

134

135

136

134
Henri van de Velde
Antwerp 1863–1957 Zurich
A garden in Kalmthout, c. 1892
Canvas, 70 × 95.5 cm
Inv. no. 12988
Acquired from the estate of the
artist in 1959

Around 1890–93, the artist often
used to stay at the Villa
Vogelenzang, the house in
Kalmthout that his brother-in-law
and sister occupied and where he
produced this picture.

135
Paul Signac
Paris 1863–1935 Paris
S. Maria della Salute, c. 1905
Signed
Canvas, 73.5 × 92.5 cm
Inv. no. 14758
Given in 1982 by Marcella Wolff in
memory of her parents Dr. Alfred
Wolff and Hanna Wolff-Josten

This painting depicts the famous
church in Venice at the beginning
of the Grand Canal, diagonally
opposite the palace of the Doges.
In the early years of the twentieth
century Signac travelled frequently
to Venice and made many
preparatory studies for the picture.

136
Claude Monet
Paris 1840–1926 Giverny
Water lillies, c. 1915
Marked with the executor's stamp
Canvas, 140 × 185 cm
Inv. no. 14562
Acquired on the London art market
in 1978

This depicts part of the water lily
pond that Monet had incorporated
into his estate at Giverny, and
which, in 1902, he decided to
rebuild. Monet planned his water
lily pictures as large-scale decorative
ensembles. By 1897–98 he was
already making preparatory studies
for them. In 1914, when they
received Georges Clemenceau's
backing, these projects acquired
a new urgency for Monet. Over
the following years, he produced
many pictures similar to the one
in Munich.

137

138

137
Ferdinand Hodler
Bern 1853–1918 Geneva
Tired of life, 1892
Signed and dated
Canvas, 150 × 295 cm
Inv. no. 9446
Acquired in 1927 on the Munich
art market

138
Ferdinand Hodler
Bern 1853–1918 Geneva
Student of Jena in 1813, 1908
Signed and dated
Canvas, 212 × 92 cm
Inv. no. 8643
Acquired in 1912 from Professor
Freiherr von Bissing as part of the
Tschudi donation

This was a full-scale study for part
of Hodler's fresco, *The March of the
Jena students in 1813 in the struggle for
freedom against Napoleon*, which he
undertook for Jena University.

139
Édouard Vuillard
Cuiseaux 1868–1940 La Baule
In the café, c. 1903
Signed
Paper, 120 × 107 cm
Inv. no. 13072
Acquired in 1960 on the art market
in Switzerland

140
Pierre Bonnard
Fontenay-aux-Roses 1867–1947 Le
Cannet
The lignite mine in Terrenoire, c. 1916
Signed
Canvas, 242 × 337 cm
Inv. no. 13721
Acquired from Frédéric Bonnard in
1966

This picture was commissioned by
Thadée Natanson, who wrote essays
on Bonnard's art and, besides his
other concerns, probably ran the
lignite mine shown here. From the
outset the picture was intended as a
large-scale wall decoration.

139

141

141
Maurice Denis
Granville 1870–1943 Paris
Celtic goddess (Epona), c. 1905
Signed
Board, 80 × 68 cm
Inv. no. 8654
Given in 1912 by Eduard Arnhold
and Robert von Mendelssohn as
part of the Tschudi donation

Epona was the Celtic goddess of
horses and other beasts of burden.

142
Odilon Redon
Bordeaux 1840–1916 Paris
The stained-glass window, c. 1912
Signed
Canvas, 92.5 × 73.5 cm
Inv. no. 13080
Acquired in 1960 from a private
collection in Switzerland

142

143

143

Fernand Khnopff

Schloss Grembergen 1858–1921
Brussels
I lock my door upon myself, 1891
Signed and dated
Canvas, 72 × 140 cm
Inv. no. 7921
Acquired from the artist in 1893

The title and subject of the picture
are taken from the seventh line of
the poem *Who shall Deliver Me?*,
written in 1864 by Christina
Georgina Rossetti, sister of the Pre-
Raphaelite painter. During 1891,
Khnopff had met the Pre-Raphaelite
painters in England.

144

Franz von Stuck

Tettenweis 1863–1928 Munich
Sin, 1893
Signed
Canvas, 88.4 × 53 cm
Inv. no. 7925
Given in 1895 by E. J. Haniel

Between 1891 and 1912, Stuck
painted many versions of this
picture, in response to its success
with the public.

145

Max Klinger

Leipzig 1857–1920 Grossjena
Elsa Asenijeff, c. 1900
Parian marble with traces of colour
(skin), inset opals (eyes), Pyrenean
marble (hair), polychrome marble
of unknown origin (drapery),
92 cm high
Inv. no. B.739
Given in 1981

The writer Elsa Asenijeff, née
Packeny (1868–1941), came from an
upper middle-class Austrian family
and was previously married to a
Bulgarian diplomat. In 1898, she met
Max Klinger. She became his model
and life companion, as well as the
mother of his daughter, Desirée.
They separated after almost 20
years. Elsa Asenijeff played an
important part in the Women's
Movement (*Diary of an Emancipated
Woman*, 1901), led an exuberant
independent life (trips by motorcar
and motorboats, etc.) and wrote
about Klinger's art. The use of
different sorts of marble was an
idea Klinger adopted from ancient
Roman statuary.

146

Edvard Munch

Engelhaugen (in Løten) 1863–1944
Ekely
Village street in Aasgardstrand, 1902,
Signed
Canvas, 59.8 × 75.8 cm
Inv. no. 11709
Acquired in 1953 from the Abels
Gallery, Cologne

In 1897, in Aasgardstrand, which he
had already visited more than once,
Munch bought a house, where he
spent time practically every year.
He was there in the summer of 1902,
when he made his dramatic break
with Tulla Larsen, whom he refused
to marry after a love affair that had
lasted four years.

144

145

146

147
Pablo Picasso
Malaga 1881–1973 Mouging
The fool, 1905
Signed
Bronze, green patina,
41.5 × 37 × 22.8 cm
Inv. no. FV 14
Acquired in 2001 on loan from the
Verein zur Förderung der Alten und
Neuen Pinakothek

Picasso created this piece as part of
a group of pictures of harlequins
and clowns, but it is the only
sculpture on this theme and the
first work by Picasso in the Neue
Pinakothek.

148
Auguste Rodin
Paris 1840–1917 Meudon
Helene von Nostitz, 1907/08
Marble, 54.3 × 50.5 × 28 cm
Inv. no. FV 11
Acquired in 1998 on loan from the
Verein zur Förderung der Alten und
Neuen Pinakothek

Helene von Nostitz, née von
Hindenburg (Berlin 1878–1944
Bassenheim), was a friend of Rodin
and acquainted with Rilke,
Hofmannsthal and numerous
others. Artistically talented, she
cultivated friendships with cultural
figures and wrote about them in a
number of books.

147

148

149

149
James Ensor
Ostend 1860–1949 Ostend
Still life in the studio, 1889
Signed and dated
Canvas, 83 × 113 cm
Inv. no. 13071
Acquired in 1960 from a private
collection

150

150
Gustav Klimt
Baumgarten (Vienna) 1862–1918
Vienna
Music, 1895
Signed and dated
Canvas, 37 × 44.5 cm
Inv. no. 8195
Acquired in 1901 at the eighth
international art exhibition in the
Glaspalast, Munich

This work was inspired by Greek
vase painting. Klimt used the
cithara and the vine branches to
represent two strands, the
Apollonian and the Dionysian,
which are united here in this
allegory of music. This picture may
have been a sketch for a second,
larger version, which served as an
overdoor for the music room in the
house of the Viennese industrialist
Dumba. This was destroyed in 1945.

151
Gustav Klimt
Baumgarten (Vienna) 1862–1918
Vienna
Margarethe Stonborough-
Wittgenstein, 1905
Signed and dated
Canvas, 180 × 90.5 cm
Inv. no. 13074
Acquired in 1960 from the
collection of Thomas Stonborough

Margarethe (1882–1958) was the
sister of the pianist Paul
Wittgenstein and the philosopher
Ludwig. The year this oil was
painted she married Jérôme
Stonborough.

151

BIBLIOGRAPHY

Verzeichnis der Gemälde in der neuen königl. Pinakothek zu München. Munich 1855

Katalog der Gemäldesammlung der Königl. Neuen Pinakothek in München. Munich 1900

Katalog der Königlichen Neuen Pinakothek zu München. 15. Auflage. Munich 1914

Katalog der Neuen Pinakothek zu München. Munich 1920

Katalog der Neuen Pinakothek zu München. Munich 1922

Gemälde Neuerer Meister aus der Neuen Pinakothek und Neuen Staatsgalerie zu München. Munich 1948

Kurt Martin, *Die Tschudi-Spende.* Munich 1962

Französische Meister des 19. Jahrhunderts. Ausgestellte Werke I, Neue Pinakothek und Staatsgalerie. Munich 1966

Meisterwerke der deutschen Malerei des 19. Jahrhunderts. Ausgestellte Werke II, Neue Pinakothek und Staatsgalerie. Munich 1967

Malerei der Gründerzeit (Bayerische Staatsgemäldesammlungen, Neue Pinakothek/München, Gemäldekataloge VI). Horst Ludwig (ed.). Munich 1977

Nach-Barock und Klassizismus (Bayerische Staatsgemäldesammlungen, Neue Pinakothek/München, Gemäldekataloge III). Barbara Hardtwig (ed.). Munich 1978

Neue Pinakothek. Erläuterungen zu den ausgestellten Werken. Munich 1981

Erich Steingräber, *Die Neue Pinakothek München.* Munich 1981

Festgabe zur Eröffnung der Neuen Pinakothek in München am 28. März 1981. Munich 1981

Museum: Neue Pinakothek München. Brunswick 1981

Christoph Heilmann, *Neue Pinakothek München.* Munich and Zürich 1984

Spätromantik und Realismus (Bayerische Staatsgemäldesammlungen, Neue Pinakothek/München, Gemäldekataloge V). Barbara Eschenburg (ed.). Munich 1984

Neue Pinakothek. Erläuterungen zu den ausgestellten Werken. 5th ed., Munich 1989

Manet bis Van Gogh. Hugo Tschudi und der Kampf um die Moderne. Ausstellungskatalog Berlin and Munich 1996/97

Spätklassizismus und Romantik (Bayerische Staatsgemäldesammlungen, Neue Pinakothek/München, Gemäldekataloge IV). Munich 2003

Von Marées bis Slevogt. Deutsche Künstler 1850/1930 (Bayerische Staatsgemäldesammlungen, Neue Pinakothek/München, Gemäldekataloge VIII). Munich 2003

INDEX